In his fifteenth book, T. Lobsang Rampa writes about his wife, his cats, his friends, his views on the police, the gentlemen of the Press, Watergate, Women's Lib . . . as well as answering many questions from readers on psychic matters. Although Dr. Rampa is elderly and infirm, his extraordinary powers are undiminished, and his comments on modern living are as perceptive as ever . . . .

Also by T. Lobsang Rampa

CANDLELIGHT
THE THIRTEENTH CANDLE
THE HERMIT
FEEDING THE FLAME
LIVING WITH THE LAMA
BEYOND THE TENTH
CHAPTERS OF LIFE
YOU-FOREVER
THE SAFFRON ROBE
THE RAMPA STORY
WISDOM OF THE ANCIENTS
DOCTOR FROM LHASA
THE THIRD EYE
THE CAVE OF THE ANCIENTS

and published by Corgi Books

Twilight

T. Lobsang Rampa

CORGI BOOKS

A DIVISION OF TRANSWORLD PUBLISHERS LTD

Dedicated to
Mr. Adonay Grassai
and
Mr. Friedrich Kosin

TWILIGHT
A CORGI BOOK 0 552 09767 5

First publication in Great Britain 1975

PRINTING HISTORY
Corgi edition published 1975

Corgi Books are published by
Transworld Publishers Ltd.,
Cavendish House, 57–59 Uxbridge Road,
Ealing, London W.5.
Made and printed in the United States of America
by Arcata Graphics,
Buffalo, New York

A SPECIAL NOTE

People were writing in saying, "You should write another book." People were writing from the ends of the Earth (*I* thought the Earth was round!) saying, "But you can't stop now, you have RAISED more questions than you have answered."

I smiled complacently in my tinny old hospital bed—the one that goes "clank-squeak" every time I move my reluctant body around. ANYONE, I thought, would agree that a decrepit, antique invalid cannot manage a thirty-pound typewriter on his lap while in bed.

My old friend in Montreal, Hy Mendelson (Boss of Simon's Cameras) spoke on the telephone: "I'm sending you a new typewriter," he said, "a nine-pound one. It is MY contribution towards the new book."

I LIKE Hy Mendelson. I'd like him for a brother. LIKE A BROTHER? Yes! Then I could BEAT HIM UP. If that wretched machine comes I'll have to start the book.

Hey, it's come. The typewriter. Now to unpack it. Someone else has to do that for me now. Rustling of paper, muttered comments, and "IT" is lifted on to the bed. OUCH! OW!! Oh my!!! It is YELLOW, like a canary that has been turned into a typewriter, like a daffodil that has swallowed too much dye. Yellow. Why don't I call it "The Yellow Peril"? It has a good type, though, and it is light and handy.

So—THANK YOU, Brother Mendelson, you are a good friend and a good man. Heigh-ho, or however it is spelt, NOW I have to start the book for sure.

CHAPTER ONE

The old grey plane soared gently through the noonday sky. Years before she had been one of the Queens of Travel bearing a famous marque indeed, traversing the air lanes of the whole world, covering the globe wherever Man travelled, carrying the elite of commerce, the stars of the theatre world and the films. In those days it had been a prestige symbol to fly in a plane such as this. Now she was old and worn, a relic from a bygone age, ousted by screaming jets and the insane desire to "get there" faster and faster for—why? What DO people do with all the time they "save"?

The old twin-engines murmured softly, a pleasant enough sound, like giant bees on a summer day. Now the old plane was on a placid routine flight from Vancouver to Calgary. Last week, perhaps, she may have been flying in the Northern Territories where the temperature was far, far below zero, and the blinding snow would make anything but instrument flight impossible. Next week, maybe, she would take oil prospectors to some of the remote oil sands in the search for more and more power by a power-mad nation, for a power-mad world. But now the former Queen of the Air was a charter plane, a poor old hack going anywhere at the whim of any customer with a few dollars to spare.

Soon the foothills of the Rockies came into view rising, ever rising, until they soared into the highest peaks of that immense range stretching across the world. Now the air was becoming turbulent and the plane bounced and tossed amid the snow-clad ranges, for here was the region where the snow never left the highest mountain peaks.

Miss Taddy Rampa uttered a yowl of outraged protest and looked as though her last moment had come. Miss Cleo Rampa swallowed hard and put on her bravest I-Can-Take-It look as she opened wide her big blue eyes as she stared hard at the rocky ground so far below.

But why the flight? Why yet another move? It all started a few months before in Vancouver——

June in Vancouver is usually such a pleasant month, a month when Nature starts to come fully awake and the weather is good, and when the sea has a smiling sparkle, when people are busy with their boats. Tourists start coming, and it is usually a time when all the storekeepers are sharpening up their wits hoping to match those of the tourists. But this June, this day in June, was not so good after all. You'll have had the same type of day, one of those days when everything—but EVERYTHING—goes wrong. Still, you are lucky, you know, you have those days every so often, or, as the saying goes, "Once in a blue moon." But supposing this type of day lasted for weeks, for months, or even for years, supposing there were patterns? Probably most people who are "in the public eye" get trouble with the moronic few who seem to exist solely to cause trouble for others.

A bus driver friend of mine told me that he and his fellows are always being persecuted by frigid old biddies who think that they are the "Lords Anointed" and are entitled to special consideration from bus drivers—they think the buses are their own private chariots. And when a bus driver politely points out that the buses are for the use of everyone the old biddy will rush off to complain and try to lose the bus driver his job. Authors get people like that to persecute them and to prevent them from being complacent or self-satisfied. I was going to tell you all about a series of events which caused me to leave British Columbia, but—conditions decreed otherwise—

The old Author sat in his wheelchair and watched complacently while a typescript was being bundled up. Another book finished, the fifteenth this time, and the old man, just out from the hospital, was smiling to himself with satisfaction because this was a book which would stir no controversy, this was a book which a publisher could take without having any qualms, without having any urgent stirrings in those lower regions and to which publishers seem to be remarkably prone.

The typescripts—for another country also was interested—were taken away to be mailed, and the old Author went about the rather difficult task of everyday living in the hope that soon he would be able to consider yet another book as had been asked for by so many interested readers.

Time went on, as it usually does, and eventually there came a gloomy message from the Agent in England saying that the typescript was not suitable for England. It seemed a fantastic state of affairs to the old Author because as was usually the case he had had the typescript read by a panel of twelve people to make sure there was nothing which could ruffle even the tenderest feathers, and all twelve had insisted that this was perhaps the most peaceful book and the "smoothest" book. But the Great God Publisher who sat upon the Golden Throne and wielded a whip laden with old lead type did not like the book. Although the matter had already been dealt with this time the edict came down from "the One Above" that apparently there must be nothing about police, sex, prisons, abortions, religion—well, there mustn't be anything about all the things I had written about. So it caused quite a problem.

At about that same moment there came a cable from another publisher who was highly elated with the book. He was well satisfied, he cabled to say that he wanted to sign the contract then and there. And another publisher expressed his interest in the book without any alterations. So it seems that in this year and age the English people appear to have rather tender susceptibilities. But we mustn't go on about this. I am told the publisher wants questions answered, so let's get on with some of those, shall we?

Hey, that's a nice little question, a sensible one, too; "Why do people sleepwalk?"

Well, just about everyone does astral travel when they go to sleep. The astral body goes off, and the physical body is meant to remain more or less passive, twisting and turning a bit, of course, in order that muscles may not be strained by being contracted for too long in one position. But sometimes a person who is in the astral will be so engrossed in his or her activities in that astral stage that he or she will unconsciously relinquish part of the control suppressing the activities of the physical back on Earth. And so the physical tends by "sympathetic reaction" to follow the astral body, and so we get a case of somnambulism, or sleep walking. The person gets out of bed and just ambles about, and it is better not to awaken such a person because if he is awakened then the sudden shock can bring back the astral body with yet another shock which makes the combination of astral and physical quite bilious. Sleep walkers who have suddenly been awakened will certainly agree with me on that point.

Another question is, "Is the Land of the Golden Light a fourth dimensional world?"

Well, yes it is a fourth dimensional world while we are in this third dimensional world. But when we are in the fourth dimensional world the Land of the Golden Light will be in the fifth dimensional world, and so on. You see, when you move upwards the stage above you is always more golden, that is, it has a more tenuous atmosphere and a higher frequency of oscillation (why don't I just call it "vibration"?).

Somebody is quite interested in this fourth dimensional world because he says, "When you die to the fourth dimensional world where does your astral body go?"

You always have to have a body, after all, think how stupid you would be if you were trying to get about and you hadn't got a body of any kind, if you were just pure thought. It wouldn't be much good to you, would it? So down here on Earth we have a physical body. Now if you can imagine what we were like on the second dimension, then what is now our physical body would then have approximated to the astral body. So we moved from the second dimension into the third, which is on this Earth, and then we occupied more solidly the Earth body which was in effect the astral body of the second dimension. So when we leave this Earth we shall vacate our Earth body and then we shall go to the astral world and live in the astral body which is then our physical body. Do you follow that? Wherever we are at that moment we have a physical body, and, of course, on each stage our body will be absolutely as solid as all those other bodies which are around us. We build up energy for a new astral body from what we are doing on what is at that moment our "Earth", or the world of our physical existence, so that eventually when you get to the—oh, what shall I say?—

eighth dimension, you will have to live in the eighth dimensional physical body while your actions and your life force will generate the ninth physical body which then, of course, will be your astral. And that astral body will be in close touch with your Overself which is much, much, much higher.

Here's another question about astral travelling. It is, "When you are astral travelling how do you go about finding the zones in which astral cats, dogs, horses, etc., live?"

Well, you don't have to go about finding it. If you are a lover of some particular animal that animal will come to your own "zone" and will actually invite you to come and visit him or her in his or her own district or hometown. Remember that when you get beyond this Earth things are very very different. Animals are not just stupid creatures who can't talk and can't do anything. Actually, humans are the dumb clucks because animals can and do talk by telepathy. Humans for the most part have to make uncouth sounds which they term a language, whereas any animal can do telepathy in any language!

To make it clearer I will say that if you want to go to a particular zone and you have a right, or a reason, to be in that particular zone, you can get there merely by thinking about it. It's as simple as that.

Well, I thought, as I said before, that we would move from British Columbia. We had had a lot of difficulty in that Province and so it is always good to go to new places, and that is what we decided to do.

The Government of British Columbia didn't help either. The Income Tax people were persecuting me wanting to know why I claimed an allowance on a wheelchair; does a person sit in a wheelchair all day for the pleasure of it? And wheelchairs wear out. So the

12

stupid asses of the Income Tax people got an "earful" from me, and I had to get three Medical Certificates, two from Montreal and one from Vancouver, to say that I had been using a wheelchair for years and was not using one for pleasure. So, all things considered, we came to the definite conclusion that the sooner we got out of Vancouver the better for our health and our peace of mind. We thought and thought, and looked at maps, and then for some quite unknown reason we settled on Alberta.

From the data we were able to get we found that Edmonton was too cold and too windy and too insular. Lethbridge, nearer the American border, was too much of a farming community where the word "insular" probably would not even be known. So we settled on Calgary.

The local airlines were not at all helpful. They were not interested in taking a disabled person in a wheelchair and two Siamese cats. So we went into the matter very thoroughly, we worked out costs of fares, we wondered whether we should get an ambulance to drive me from Vancouver to Calgary, and eventually with the help of a friend we managed to get in touch with a very good Air Charter firm. We were able to settle for a quite reasonable sum for the trip which compared very favourably indeed with what it would have cost by ambulance by road.

The Great Day came and at last our lease was terminated. I trundled aboard a thing known as a Handi-Bus, a thing which has a ramp up which a wheelchair is pushed into a sort of empty truck or bus, and there the wheelchair is strapped very securely to the floor, the ramp is folded up outside the back, and friends or relatives of the victim get into a taxi and then the cavalcade moves off. We went through Vancouver to Vancouver Airport. There we met the first obstacle.

13

It had been arranged that a forklift should be available to lift me complete with electrically-powered wheelchair into the big old plane. Well, the forklift wasn't there, at that part of the Airport they didn't have one! I sat there in the back of the Handi-Bus, and eventually I got fed up with the whole idea so while people were milling around discussing what they should do, how to get me and the wheelchair in the plane, I moved forward in the chair to the foot of the ladder leading up into the body of the plane. There I managed to pull myself into the plane by the power of my arms alone. My legs are nothing to boast about, but with my arms I could still toss a heavy man over my shoulders—it would probably give me a heart attack it would be worth it!

So I got myself into that old plane, and with crutches managed to move to a seat along one side. Then a load of men lifted the wheelchair into place, and the others of the little party got in, together with the luggage. The plane roared and roared, and eventually we got clearance from the Airport and rushed down the runway and leapt into the air. And some of these old planes do indeed leap into the air.

We took a climbing turn over the harbour and then made a 300 degree turn toward the Rockies.

The mountains were beautiful. Cleo was fascinated in looking about her. Taddy was continually distressed at the thought that if there were any more bumps she might lose her lunch, always Taddy's first thought. And it is not so easy for an aging Girl Cat to find her "air-going legs" when the plane is bouncing and jouncing all over the sky.

The time dragged slowly by, it always seems such a waste sitting in a plane doing nothing except look out, and all the time beneath us there were the cruel jagged rocks with their high points enrobed in snow, and lower down their flanks the vivid blue of deep, deep water. Occasionally there was a sight of a small farming community served by a minute airstrip, or the sight of float planes taking off from those mountain lakes where no airstrip could be managed.

The light came on and the sign lit up, "Fasten seat belts—no smoking." Well, no smoking didn't apply to us, but we fastened our seat belts and grabbed hold of the cats who, for safety, we now put in baskets.

The plane slanted down, passed through a layer of cloud, and then we emerged over the foothills on the other side of the Rockies. Below us was the Foothills Hospital which a year later I was to enter as a patient. To the left of us was the big University of Calgary. The plane swooped on getting lower and lower. We looked with interest at the city which was going to be our new home; we saw the Calgary Tower, we saw the skyscrapers of downtown, and we saw the twisting river, or perhaps it should be rivers—the Bow and the Elbow—as they threaded a labyrinthine way through the city, down from the mountains and on toward Lethbridge, rivers so silted up that they were not able to be used by pleasure boats because of the eddies, because of the sandbanks—and because the Police didn't want the rivers to be used!

Below us the Airport loomed. The pilot nodded his head in satisfaction and the plane tilted even more steeply. There came the juddering rumble as the wheels met the runway and speeded up. Soon the tail dropped and we trundled along gently into the area of the charter company.

Here conditions were different. Everything was ready. As soon as the plane came to a stop in front of the offices an elderly gentleman drove a forklift truck to the side of the old plane and the pilot and co-pilot grabbed me and my wheelchair quite tightly as though they feared that I might escape or fall out or something. But I am used to wheelchair managing, and I soon drove out through the door of the plane and straight on to the forklift platform, but even here I was secured; the pilot and the co-pilot held on to me and held on to the sides of the forklift while gently we were lowered to the ground.

The question of payment. Ah! We always have to pay for our jaunts, do we not? And so it was that first we paid for our trip and then another Handi-Bus backed to a stop in front of me. The ramp was lowered with a fearsome rattle, and I drove my wheelchair up into the body. And then the rains came down! It rained harder at that moment and for the rest of that day than it has rained at any time since in Calgary. We had a wet welcome.

Once again my wheelchair was very securely strapped to the floor. All our luggage was slung in and then we roared off along the Airport road, over the river bridge, and into the city of Calgary itself. By now the rush-hour traffic was starting and the rain was coming down harder and harder. Eventually we reached our destination and a group of people rushed out, grabbed our luggage and rushed inside into the shelter of the building. Slowly the driver unshackled the chair from all its restraints and I drove down the ramp and into the house also. Our first sight of Calgary was a wet one.

Calgary is a friendly city, a new city, a city which has not yet grown cynical and uncaring. After a year in Calgary I can say—yes, it is a nice place indeed for people who can get about, but there are disadvantages; the curbs here are very high indeed, not suitable for wheelchair users, and the roads too have a very great camber so that a wheelchair tends to run toward the gutter all the time. The next question I am going to answer is one I don't want to answer, but one which I have had great pressure to answer. It is about the hollow Earth.

But first—before you all start writing to me about *quis custodiet ipsos custodes* let me say my bit about the Crummy Cops who RUIN our civilization. Ready? Then here it is:

"Who has custody of the custodians?" Who polices the police? "Absolute power corrupts." But does not the police now have "absolute power"? And ARE they corrupt?

The Law states that a person is deemed innocent until *proved* guilty; the police automatically regard everyone as GUILTY!

A person has the right to be confronted by his accuser, yet the police do not even tell a person of what he IS accused until they, by trickery, have forced him to admit *something*.

In my personal opinion the police are out of touch; no one likes policemen—they live isolated in their barracks or in their secluded groups aloof from those they should know. There is no substitute for the old fashioned Man on the Beat.

An old Irish policeman, who is a very dear friend, pounded his beat for years before he retired. He KNEW everyone in his area, and could prevent troubles before they became serious. He was an unpaid family counsellor, giving advice, friendly warnings, and only "taking in" an offender when it became really essential. He had—and has—the respect and affection of the whole community.

The old-type policeman was welcomed into the houses on his beat. Now—policemen stay enclosed in their cars ... and lose touch with people.

Now the police divide the world into two classes, the

17

"goodies" and the "baddies," with the police only being the "goodies."

A few years ago the police were courteous, considerate and helpful. Then a policeman making an enquiry would say, "Ah then, Mrs. Blank, and can I see the Good Man? I hear he's been after the poteen a bit too much. Sleeping it off, is he? Then I'll call around later."

Now the police move in pairs, as if afraid to move alone. Now they thrust their way in without any regard whatever for the conditions and circumstances. "R.C.M.P." they mutter, shoving a badge at one, and entering uninvited.

"A man is innocent until proved guilty." But the police treat everyone as though he were guilty merely because he has attracted police notice! Of course, if a man was seen to kill another, then naturally let the police "go in shooting." Surely, though, in routine enquiry matters, the police should show tact? What if an invalid is in the bathroom or having treatment, do the police HAVE to force their unwelcome way in? They DO—we know that from personal experience!

The police are now hated, isolated, living in a dream of colourful uniforms, horse manure and stamping feet. It is time to re-organise them, show them that they are not God's Chosen but SERVANTS of the public.

Teach the police courtesy, politeness, manners, let them chase (and catch) criminals, and let ordinary decent law-abiding citizens alone. Only then will they regain the respect which most certainly is lacking now.

And the worst offenders, in my opinion, are the Mounties with their arrogant posturing. Like many others, having been senselessly harassed by the police, *I* say, "Help the police? No sir! I would not do a THING to help them—they TURN on you!" And they HAVE!!

18

CHAPTER TWO

Mr.—no, perhaps it would be better not to give his name. Let me instead say a "gentleman" wrote to me saying, "I've read some of your advertisements in your novels saying as how you'll answer any question on any subject free of charge. Well, okay, that's fine by me. I've paid hundreds of dollars to people who advertised that they would answer questions but they've never given me a satisfactory answer. But you're begging people to write to you so what have I got to lose?"

Well, I thought to myself, this poor fellow makes a lot of mistakes, doesn't he? In the first case I have never written a novel in my life. A novel is fiction. I write only truth and nothing but the truth. Then he says that I advertise that I will answer questions on any subject free of charge. Well, that's news to me. I thought I did my best to discourage idle letter writing, and never in my life have I said I would answer any question on any subject free of charge or otherwise. I know my own subjects and I pride myself I know them quite well, and I can answer such questions. Unfortunately—like this particular man —people write to me thinking that I am delighted to pay the cost of typing, postage, the cost of stationery and all that. They never think of reimbursing one for one's expenses. One might almost call them cheapskates!

Yes, it is perfectly true, though, there are certain people—fake seers—who advertise that for a few dollars or a few hundred dollars they will answer questions. Pity

I don't do something like that, it might cut down the volume of silly questions. But as this man writes questions on a subject which will come much to the forefront in the near future it might be worth looking into the matter. Now, this is what he says—in substance, of course, because his letter is no literate work at all; the way he writes he might never have been to school.

He says, in effect, "A lot of people think there may be a world inside this world. The world may be hollow. What have you got to say about that? You claim to know a lot about religion. How come you never mention such a thing? How come no religious book ever mentions such a thing?"

Well, he is wrong enough there because the religion or belief in which I am most informed (Buddhism) does indeed refer to an Inner World. There is a special word for it. It is called "Agharta." It is a word very frequently used in Buddhist Scripture, in fact in Tibetan lore there is much mention made of Shamballa where the King of all the world lives, the King who is hidden from the millions on the surface of the world.

Tibetans firmly believe in the King of the world living inside the world, not as some sort of demon but as an extremely good King, a good spiritual ruler who is alive in two planes at once, the physical plane where he lives for ever and ever, and the spiritual, or astral, plane where similarly he lives for ever and ever.

Tibetans believe that the King of the world gave his first instructions to the first Dalai Lama and the Dalai Lama was, in fact, the outer world representative of the inner world King.

Certainly there are tunnels in Tibet which go deeper and deeper and deeper, and there are many legends about strange people coming up through those tunnels and holding converse with Lamas of high degree. As I have written in some of my books I have been in some of those tunnels, and I have also been in some of those tunnels in Ultima Thule. There are certain places in the Earth where it is possible for the Initiate to travel down into the centre of the Earth and meet representatives of that inner civilization, and among quite a number of people there is a definite knowledge that people from the inner world do come out to converse with those on the surface. Actually, of course, some of the U.F.O.'s come from this inner world.

There are, then, tunnels from Tibet to the inner world and tunnels from Brasil to the inner world. Brasil and Tibet are two vitally important parts of the outer world which have a special attraction for the Inner People.

It is a most unfortunate thing that there are so many superstitious beliefs which have never been properly investigated because it is known to a few "sensitives" that there is a tunnel beneath the Greater Pyramids. Now, by Pyramid I am not referring exclusively to the Pyramids in Egypt, there are many more than that. All these Pyramids used to be marker beacons sending messages to the Gardeners of the Earth and their representatives who traverse space in their spaceships. There are Pyramids in Egypt and in certain parts of South America, also there are very important Pyramids in the Gobi Desert but the Gobi Desert, being controlled by Communist China nowadays, not so much is known about that to the outside world. All these Pyramids are connected to the inner world, and in the days of the Pharaohs many of the magical rites of Egypt were conducted by people who came up out of their inner world specifically for that purpose.

But, to get back to basics again, according to the Buddhist religious books there were vast convulsions upon the Earth and the climates of the countries of the Earth changed and changed and changed, and as they changed tribes of people were driven from cold zones into warmer zones and during one such excursion—about 25,000 years ago—a tribe of people emerged on to what would now be called the North Pole. They kept on walking and walking and eventually they found that they had the sun always ahead of them, never behind, never rising or setting. Eventually in course of time they found that they were inside the Earth, they found that the Earth was hollow and they settled there. It is thought, too—I should have put this in brackets!—that all the Gypsies came from inside the Earth.

I have heard many people discussing a hollow Earth and the opponents of the theory always say "Well, if there is a hollow Earth how is it that commercial airlines which fly over the North Pole do not see the opening; commercial planes nowadays do indeed fly over the North Pole and perhaps the South Pole, too, and if there was a big opening in the Earth then obviously the pilots would see such an opening."

That is not true, you know. Commercial airlines do not fly over the North Pole, nor do they fly over the South Pole; they fly quite a distance away for the simple reason that if they did indeed fly over the Poles it would interfere very seriously with their navigational instruments, and so commercial flights are always routed so that the mythical North or South Pole is avoided by many many miles and thus interference with the compasses also is obviated.

Then there are others who say, "Well, all these explorers who have been to the North Pole or to the South Pole, if there had been a hole in the Earth they would have found that hole." But then again, no, it's not true, no one has been to the North Pole, no one has been to the South Pole. We get reports of people who have got somewhere near such-and-such a Pole and have gone on for many miles, in other words they have been more or less lost. Ancient history, and modern history too, teaches us that often sailors will spot debris floating from the Poles (I use "Poles" just to conform and make the location obvious). There are also floating animals or birds. Now, everyone knows that you don't get birds and insects flying at the North Pole or the South Pole, you don't get green leaves floating, so where do they come from? From inside the Earth, of course.

I believe this; supposing one had a vehicle and one could journey from here—wherever you are at the moment is "here"—to the North Pole you would go on and on and you would reach what you would believe to be the location of the North Pole, and then you would continue on and eventually you would find yourself with a different sort of sun above you. The sun being an atomic sort of thing occurring naturally not merely in the centre of this Earth but in many other worlds as well. Astronomers have found that on the Moon, for instance, there are strange lights seen at times about the Poles. You might say, "Oh yes, but men have been to the Moon." Sure they have, but they have been to a very limited spot on the Moon, a spot, a circle, of about five miles radius. Oh no, they haven't explored the Moon, and they haven't explored this Earth. There is quite a lot of this Earth which still has to be explored.

If you are interested and if you go to your Public Library I am sure you can find many books dealing with an inner Earth and stories of people who have been lost and then have sailed on into a strange world, and eventually they have found themselves just inside the inner world. Better than the Library, buy some books at a good bookstore.

People have asked me to explain whatever such a world could look like, how can there be a world which is hollow inside? The best way I can explain it is like this:—

Imagine you have a coconut. The outside of the coconut is the outer Earth. And remember this, that if your hands are hot the moisture which you have deposited on the outside of the coconut in merely touching it is equal to the depth of the deepest sea on this, the full size Earth. That's a thought worth bearing in mind.

Anyway, you've got your coconut and you are looking at the outer side of it. That represents our conventional Earth. Now, make a hole in the part known as the eyes, and make another hole in the part right opposite the eyes. You can liken these to the North and the South Poles. You should make the hole about an inch in diameter and let out all the milk. Then you have the outer hard shell which is the crust of the Earth, and inside you have the white flesh of the coconut which represents the inner world surface. Right in the middle of the coconut you have to somehow fix a flashlight bulb to represent the ever-burning inner sun.

Now—the hard shell which is the crust and the softer inner side which provides footing for inner worlders provides, also, the source of gravity which keeps people feet down on the upper surface and feet down on the inner surface. There is no evidence whatever that the inner surface of the Earth is molten gas or molten iron or molten rock or molten anything else. That has just been a supposition of "scientists" who have made many other false suppositions like when they said that if a man travelled at more than 30 miles an hour his lungs would burst with the air pressure. And like when they said that it would be impossible for any spaceship to land on the Moon because it would sink right into the impalpable dust. Oh no, scientists are merely guessers with a University education. Often they are worse guessers than people without a University education because scientists are taught that if this person or that person says a thing is impossible then it is indeed impossible, and so instead of being taught to think they are just being taught to think that Author So-and-So is infallible and if he says a thing is impossible then indeed it is.

I believe that people inside the Earth are very very highly evolved people indeed who are remnants from Lemuria, Mu, Atlantis, and many even older civilizations. The Earth has been wracked by cataclysms, storms, meteors and all the rest of it, and often people on the surface have been decimated yet inside life goes on serenely, untroubled by things that are happening outside and so spirituality and scientific knowledge has progressed.

You may not be aware that the Chileans, who have a great interest in the South Pole areas, have photographed U.F.O.'s rising out of that territory. Most interesting pictures were taken by a geophysical team of Chilean scientists. Unfortunately, under considerable pressure, those photographs were turned over to the U.S.A. authorities ... and that is the last that has been heard of them.

U.F.O.'s are of different types, but one type comes from inside the Earth, and there are many U.F.O.'s seen nowadays because the Inner People are greatly worried by the atomic explosions taking part on the outer surface of the Earth. After all, if the explosion is big enough then perhaps the crust of the Earth will be cracked even worse than it is at present and the whole Earth will perish. That is why the Inner People are so concerned, why they are trying to control atomic research on this world.

Have you really studied the journeys of explorers who claim they have been to the North Pole or to the South Pole? Without any exception they report that they found the temperature rising as they travelled north, they found more open seas than they expected, they found many things which were completely at variance with the North Pole or South Pole theory where things got colder and colder as the Poles were approached. Actually the Poles do not exist except as some mythical symbol up in the air, perhaps in the centre of the opening leading into the Earth.

The aurora borealis could easily be the reflections from the inner sun when conditions are suitable, or they could even be radiations from the nuclear life within your world.

But someone is sure to say all this is impossible, of course there is no hole leading into the Earth, the idea is absurd—ridiculous. If there was a whacking great hole at the North Pole and another at the South Pole then obviously air pilots would have seen them, astronauts would have seen the holes also, and in fact anyone looking would be able to see right through the Earth just the same as one can see daylight through the other end of a blown egg. No, someone is sure to say, this author has gone round the bend at last . . . if he didn't go round years ago.

That attitude is all wrong, you know. It shows that the person doesn't know the facts. How many of you have been to the North Pole? How many of you have been to the South Pole? How many of you know climatic conditions there? What about cloud coverage, for example? What about viewing conditions? No, Critical Reader, I haven't gone round the bend—you have if you think that all this is impossible; if you think all this is impossible then you are not merely around the bend, you are cantering along the home straight which is a darn sight worse.

Think how in well populated areas great caves have remained hidden for hundreds or thousands of years. Look at the cave in which the Dead Sea Scrolls were found. That cave was only found completely by accident.

Look at Canada. Great areas of Quebec have not been explored. And supposing a plane flew over certain of these areas in Quebec which would be covered with ice most of the year, then photographs might show reflections precisely as it should show reflections from snow and ice. Or the photographs may show dark patches precisely as they could show dark patches of snow and ice. Ice can be of many different colours, you know, it is not all white and tinselly like you put on Christmas trees. You can even get red snow in certain areas; I know that because I have seen it. But the whole point is that a photograph taken over the approximate location of the North Pole or the South Pole might show strange shadows, but if people had no reason to investigate the shadows then they wouldn't go there and probe, would they? It takes a lot of money too to mount an expedition to the mythical North Pole or the equally mythical South Pole. It takes a lot of money, it takes a special breed of man, it takes a lot of back-up supplies, and it takes a big bank account to pay the insurance!

But back to Canada; many, many areas in the Northern Territories have not been explored. Some areas have never even been seen by humans. How do you know what holes there are in the Northern Territories when no one has been there? It is stupid to say these things are

27

impossible until you know all the facts, until you are an expert in photography, until you are an expert in geology.

Think of astronauts or cosmonauts, or whatever the current term for them is; well, then they are taking off and are reasonably close to the Earth presumably they have something else to do besides look for a hole where the North Pole or South Pole should be, and in the Polar regions the viewing is often horribly unsatisfactory, fogs, snow-storms, confusing reflections from snow, ice and water. It's worth noticing also that when astronauts are in orbit they have specific tasks to do, taking a peep at the Russians, taking an even harder look at the Chinese. Are there telltale shadows which indicate that silos have been erected which could be the starting point of inter-continental ballistic missiles? And if so, in which direction are the silos inclined? By knowing things like this the Americans can tell if the war lords of Pekin have rockets aimed at New York or Los Angeles, or somewhere else. They have to take into account the degree of inclination and the rotation of the Earth so that they can then forecast to within just a few miles the target area of the I.C.B.M.'s. The Americans are much more interested in knowing what the Russians, the Poles, the Chinese and the Czechs are doing than finding out something about a hole in the Earth. Some of the Americans, for instance, would be more interested in checking a hole in the head than a hole in the Earth!

So you can take it that unless there are very special conditions and very special circumstances these particular openings in the Earth would not be photographed, and as for thinking that you could look in one end and see out through the other just as you would through a straight railway tunnel—well, that idea is crazy. You couldn't do it. Think of a railway tunnel absolutely dead straight. You look in one end and if you are very very careful you might possibly see a little dot of light at the other end, and that railway tunnel may be not even half a mile long. We, if we were looking through a hole in the Earth, would have to look at something which was nearly eight thousand miles long. That is, the tunnel through which you would be looking (through the Earth) would be so long that you just wouldn't see any light at the other end. Not only that but even if you had such good sight that you could see all the way through and distinguish a small hole, then you would still be looking at darkness because unless the sun was opposite you would have no light-reflection, would you?

If you are going to deny the POSSIBILITY of there being a hollow Earth then you are just as bad as the people who think that the world is flat! In passing I wonder how the "Flat-Earth Society" in London, England, explains some of the astronauts' photographs now. As far as I am aware there is still a society in England who swear on a stack of comics (must be comics!) that the world is flat and all the photographs have been faked. I read something about it and had a good laugh, and I wish I could remember where I read the article. Anyway, if you are not sure why not keep an open mind then you won't be caught short when the proof is forthcoming?

There is another thing you have to consider; the Governments of the world, or rather the Governments of the super powers, are nearly killing themselves to hush up everything about U.F.O.'s. Why? Millions of people have seen U.F.O.'s. I was reading an article only yesterday in which it was said that statistics prove that 15 million Americans have seen U.F.O.'s. So if 15 million in one country alone have seen them then it's a sure thing that there must be something like U.F.O.'s. Argentina, Chile, and other sensible countries acknowledge the existence of U.F.O.'s. They don't necessarily understand what they are or why they are, but they acknowledge them and that is a big step forward.

The Governments hush up and conceal all the truth about U.F.O.'s; now—supposing the American Government, for example, had photographs of U.F.O.'s entering or leaving the Earth, supposing they had definite proof that the Earth was hollow and that there was a high civilization within, then quite without a doubt the Governments would try to conceal knowledge of the truth or people would panic, start looting, commit suicide, and do all the strange things that humans do when they panic. We have only to remember the Orson Welles—Raiders from Mars—radio broadcast of a few years ago when Americans really did most thoroughly panic in spite of being told by the announcers that it was only a play.

So—the Governments conceal the truth because they are afraid of panic. But perhaps in the not too distant future they will have to admit the truth, the truth being that there is a hollow Earth and a highly intelligent race within that hollow Earth, and that one form of U.F.O. comes from inside the hollow Earth. Mind you there is more than one type of U.F.O. One type comes from "outer space", another type comes from "inner space", that is, the inner side of the Earth.

But again, supposing you say, "I still say the fellow's crazy because there wouldn't be any room for a civilization inside the Earth." Well sir or madam, as the case may be, that implies that YOU haven't done your homework. Let's have a look at some figures. I am not going to quote exact figures or someone is sure to say, "Oh look at him, now we know that he's a fraud, he's 6 inches short in

30

the diameter of the world"! Oh yes, Loving Reader, people do write and say such things, and they think themselves very clever, But anyway, let's have some rough figures.

Now, the diameter of the Earth is roughly seven thousand nine hundred and twenty-seven miles. Now, supposing we say (we've got to give some figures, haven't we?) that the thickness of the crust of the Earth on the Earth side and the thickness of the "soil" side of the inner Earth comes to eight hundred miles. Well, if you add those two eight hundred's together you get one thousand six hundred, and if you subtract that from seven thousand nine hundred and twenty-seven you get six thousand three hundred and twenty-seven miles. That, then, we can say is very very approximately the diameter of the world inside this world.

That means that the inner world is (again roughly) 2.9 times larger than the Moon, so that if somehow you could get the Moon inside the Earth the poor wretched thing would rattle around like the pea inside a referee's whistle. The diameter of the Moon, remember, is roughly two thousand one hundred and sixty miles, and the estimated diameter of the world inside this Earth is, we decided, six thousand three hundred and twenty-seven miles. So now YOU do some arithmetic for a change. I'm right, aren't I?

Another point of interest is this; only an eighth of the surface of the world is land, seven-eighths is water—seas, oceans, lakes, and all that, so it could easily be that there is more land INSIDE the world than outside, and if there is more land inside then there could be more people inside. Or if they regularly take "the Pill" they may have bred for quality rather than quantity.

I believe all this, you know, I have believed it for

years, and I have studied it very very thoroughly. I have read all I could about it, and if you do the same then without a doubt you will come to the same conclusion that I have which is that there is another world inside this Earth of ours, that it is 2.9 times the size of the Moon, and that it is populated by a very intelligent race.

Another thing of interest is this; look at all the explorers who have been "to the Pole". None of them has ever PROVED that he got there. Think of Admiral Peary, think of Wilkinson, Amundsen, Shackleton, Scott, etc., etc. All these men who, in theory went there by water or went there on foot or who flew to the area—not one of them ever truly, demonstrably proved that he had reached the Pole itself. I believe they couldn't because "the Pole" is a remote area somewhere in space above the surface, and, as has been proved, the location varies quite a lot.

So there it is. If you are interested don't write to me about it because I have said all I am going to say about it. Oh yes, I know a lot more, I know a great deal more than I have written, but just trot along to a really good bookstore and BUY some books on the hollow Earth. It is kinder to the author to buy than to read it up in the Public Library because the poor wretched author has to live and he can't live when people just read stuff free. He depends upon his royalties. After all, if it's worth reading it's worth paying for.

CHAPTER THREE

It was cold in Calgary. Snow lay all about obscuring the railway tracks, covering the frozen river. The cold was terrible, a cold that seemed to penetrate everywhere, a cold which seemed to magnify sound from the frozen streets. Drivers still whirled along seemingly without a care in the world. Calgary, we are told, has two claims to fame; it has more cars per capita—why not say "per person"?—than any other place on the North American continent. And the second claim to fame, if fame it can be called, is that the drivers of Calgary are more dangerous than any other drivers on the North American continent. People run around as if they hadn't a care in the world. Then, presumably, they wake up in Heaven or the Other Place and find that they have, they've got a load of kharma from the people they killed in the accident!

But the cold this day was just fantastic. And then across the sky there came a peculiar band of cloud, or should I say cloud and light intermixed, and the air immediately grew warmer as if someone "Up There" had taken pity on the poor mortals of Calgary and switched on a very efficient electric heater.

The air suddenly grew warm. The crisp snow became soggy, and water poured from rooftops. The Chinook winds had come; the greatest blessing of Calgary, a special meteorological formation which suddenly brings a whole lot of hot air (well, look at their Government!) from Vancouver, hot air which turns a frigid day into a mellow day.

The snow soon melted. The Chinook winds persisted during the afternoon and evening, and on the following day there was no trace of snow at all in Calgary.

But letters do not bother to wait for warm weather, they come all the time like bills and income tax demands, they wait for no man, they wait for nothing. Here is a letter shrieking in bright fluorescent red ink. Some cantankerous lady wrote, "You tell us about Mantras, but the things you tell us are no good, your Mantras don't work. I wanted to win the Sweepstake and I said my Mantra three times, and I didn't win it. What have you to say about that?"

Well now, why do some of these old biddies get in such a state? It's shockingly bad for their blood pressure. It's far worse for their spiritual development. In any case she wasn't saying MY Mantra, she was apparently doing a thing against which I specifically warn one. It is not right to try to win a gamble by the use of Mantras. A gamble is a gamble, just that and nothing more, and if you try to use Mantras for gambling wins then you do a lot of harm to yourself.

There have been a lot of people, though, who seem to have had bad luck in not getting their Mantras in good working order. Probably it is because they don't set about it in the right way. Undoubtedly it is because they cannot visualize what it is they want to get over to the subconscious. You see, you've got to know what you are saying, you've got to convince yourself what you are saying, and having convinced yourself you've got to convince your sub-conscious. Look at it like a business proposition.

You want something specific. It must be something which your sub-conscious wants as well. Let's say for example—and this is just an idle example, remember, so

34

don't write me a load of letters saying I have contradicted myself or something like that, as so many of you absolutely delight in doing. Most times you are wrong, anyway!

Let us say that Mr. Smith wants a job and he is going to an interview tomorrow, or the day after, or the day after that with Mr. Brown. So Mr. Smith churns out a Mantra. He mumbles, mumbles, mumbles while he is thinking about getting this nonsense over so he can go to the pictures or go and get a drink or go and find a girl friend, or something like that. He tries to get it over and done with, and having said it three times he is convinced he has done everything necessary and the Powers That Be are responsible for everything else after. Then Mr. Smith rushes out, goes to the pictures, perhaps goes to a bar and gets a swig or two of beer, and picks up a girl, and when he goes for his interview with Mr. Brown— well, he doesn't make a hit. Of course he doesn't, he hasn't prepared for it, he hasn't done his homework. What he should do is this:—

Mr. Smith wants a job so he has applied for a job having assured himself that he has the necessary qualifications and abilities with which to carry out the tasks imposed by that job if he gets it. He has heard from a Mr. Brown saying that Mr. Brown will grant him an interview at such-and-such a time on such-and-such a day.

A sensible Mr. Smith tries to find out something about Mr. Brown if he can. What's the man like? What does he look like? What is his position in the firm? Is he a friendly type? Well, you can usually find out those things by phoning the telephone girl of the firm concerned and asking her. A lot of these girls are very flattered indeed. So if Mr. Smith says he is trying to get a job with the firm and he is going to be given an interview on such-and-such a day and will the girl tell him something about Mr. Brown, the interviewer—after all, he can say, I shall soon be working with you so let's make a friendship now, tell me what you can. The girl invariably responds favourably if she is approached in the right way, she is flattered that someone has appealed to her for help, she is flattered that someone thinks she is such a good judge of character, she is flattered to think that a possibly new member to the firm had sense enough to get in touch with her. So she gives the information. Perhaps she can tell Mr. Smith that a picture of Mr. Brown appeared in The Dogwashers Monthly Magazine, or something, when he took up his new appointment with the firm. So Mr. Smith goes along to the local Library and takes a good hard look at a picture of Mr. Brown. He looks at the picture and looks at it, and fixes it in his mind. Then off he goes home keeping Mr. Brown's face in his mind. There he sits down and imagines that Mr. Brown is in front of him unable to talk, the poor fellow just has to sit and listen. So Mr. Smith unloads a talk about himself, about his own abilities. He says what he has to say convincingly, and if he is alone he can say it in a low voice. If he is not alone he'd better just think it to himself otherwise some other person in the house might take Mr. Smith off to the place where "people like that" are taken, because not everyone understands visualization Mantras, etc.

If this is done right, then when Mr. Smith goes to see Mr. Brown, Mr. Brown has a distinct impression that he has seen Mr. Smith before under very favourable terms, and do you know why? I'll tell you.

If it is done properly Mr. Smith will have "made his mark in the ether", and his sub-conscious will, during the time of astral travel, meet and discuss things with Mr.

Brown's sub-conscious. Oh good gracious me, it really does work, I've tried it time after time, I know hundreds —thousands—of people who have tried it too and it does work IF YOU DO YOUR JOB PROPERLY!

But if a lazy Mr. Smith just thinks of girl chasing, film watching and beer drinking then his mind is on those things—girl chasing, film watching and beer drinking— and he doesn't get any response from Mr. Brown's sub-conscious.

I'll tell you what I'll do; I'll make a worthwhile sugges-tion to you—to those of you who find it hard to concen-trate in the right way. Now, there are such things as rosaries, Catholics have them, Buddhists have them, and a lot of others have them. Not everyone has them like hippies just for little things to hang on to them to make them look different. So let's think of a string of beads. All right, what are we going to do about the beads? First of all we have to make the type of string of beads we want. How many beads are we going to have and does it mat-ter how many beads there are? It most certainly does!

Psychiatrists are a pretty dumb lot, really, and I think most of them are crazier than the people they treat. It's like setting a thief to catch a thief. You have to get a lunatic to treat a lunatic, so to my way of thinking most psychiatrists are as crazy as can be. But sometimes, by accident, they come up with a piece of information which can be of use to someone, so a gang of these head-shrinkers have come up with an idea that it takes forty-five repetitions to get a thing safely locked into one's subconsciousness. So—for those of you who can't concen-trate on a thing properly let's have a string of beads, let's make it fifty beads for good measure. So you start off by going along to the best hobby or handicraft store you can find, and pawing through a load of loose beads until you find the type, style, pattern and size which most appeals to you. I find that the best ones for me are of average pea-size and the ones I have are of polished wood. Then you get a length of nylon cord on which the beads will very easily slide. Then you buy your fifty beads, and they must be identical in size, and then if you want to you can get about three larger ones to act as a marker. When you get home you thread fifty of your beads on this nylon thread. Make sure they slide easily. And then tie a knot, and on the two pieces of thread hanging down from the knot thread perhaps three larger beads and knot the end again. The idea of this is merely to tell you when you have completed one complete circuit of your beads. So then you sit down as comfortably as you can in a chair, or lie down, or if it is more comfortable—stand on your head. It doesn't matter how you sit or lie so long as you are comfortable and you do not have muscles under tension.

Then you decide what you want to say to your sub-conscious. Now, it is important what you say and how you say it. It just definitely, definitely must be positive, you cannot have a negative thing or you will get the wrong result. It should be "I will . . ." It should be short and sharp, and definitely something which can be repeated without too much strain on the intellect. You'd be surprised how strained some intellects become!

Mr. Smith wants to impress Mr. Brown, so he could say (this is just an example, mind—don't quote me!), "I will favourably impress Mr. Brown. I will favourably impress Mr. Brown. I will favourably impress Mr. Brown." Well, poor old Mr. Smith has to repeat that fifty times, each time as he gets to Mr. Brown in his words he flips one bead back, and so on until he has repeated fifty times. The idea is to use the beads as a form of computer because you cannot say, "I will favourably impress Mr. Brown, that's said it once, I will favourably impress Mr. Brown, that's said it twice, I will favourably impress Mr. Brown, that's said it three times," because you will get all gummed up with your words and with your instructions to your Overself.

Having decided fifty times that you are going to favourably impress Mr. Brown, then you get down to it and talk to him as if he were actually in front of you, as I have said several paragraphs ago. So that is really all there is to it.

You should handle your beads very frequently to imbue them with your personality, to make them part of you, to make sure each one slides properly, to make sure that you can flap the wretched things around without having to definitely think about moving them. It has to become second nature to you, and—if you have other people in the same house with you then the best thing you can do is to have small beads which you can keep in your pocket then you can put one hand in your pocket and move around and nobody will know what you are doing except being so slovenly—they think—that you keep your hand in your pocket all the time.

Now, once again I am going to tell you that—yes, quite definitely you can win a Sweepstake by using Mantras BUT ONLY IF YOU KNOW EXACTLY WHO IS GOING TO MAKE THE SWEEPSTAKE DRAW! If you are going to get a positive action you have to know who you are going to act upon. It's too utterly foolish for anything to say that you are going to do a Mantra for the person in charge of such-and-such a thing, that's no good. You must actually know the person who is organizing a draw or who is going to draw the ticket from the box or whatever it is. If you cannot do

39

that you cannot place any faith at all in the Mantra. It means that you must, must, MUST address your remarks to some sub-consciousness and not just fritter your energies into idle space. Is that clear?

If you know, then, that Mrs. Knickerbaum is running the raffle for the Slithering Snakes Society and the take is going to be worthwhile, then you can address your remarks to the sub-conscious entity of Mrs. Knickerbaum, and if you do it on the lines suggested in this Chapter you have a good chance of success unless someone else is doing it and they've got a bit more think-power than you have, in which case you lose out.

But a warning, there is a warning to everything, you've got to stop and give way to approaching traffic, you've got to yield here, you've got to halt there, etc., etc. Everything is a warning, so here is another one for good measure; money which has been acquired by means of a Mantra like this really brings happiness, most often it brings misery. And if you want it entirely for selfish reasons then you can be quite sure you are going to get misery. So—don't do it.

I have had letters from people saying, "Oh Dr. Rampa, I do want to win the Such-and-Such a Sweepstake, and I know you can help me. You let me win a hundred thousand dollars and I'll give you twenty per cent, that'll make it worthwhile for you, won't it? I'll give you the number of the ticket—etc., etc."

The answer is, "No madam, it is not worth my while. I do not believe in gambling, and if I go in to this with you for twenty per cent then I should be as culpable as you, and anyway madam, if I wanted to do this why should I do it for just twenty per cent from you—why shouldn't I do it myself and get the whole lot of money?"

So many people see advertisements for infallible

schemes for winning "at the horses", and they don't seem to realize that if the propounder of the infallible scheme had indeed something which was successful he wouldn't be selling the idea to someone else for a dollar or two, he would be making millions using his own infallible system. That's right, isn't it?

It might be a good idea here to say a bit more about these people who are so anxious to pray for one. I get a lot of letters from people who say that their group will be praying hard for me, etc. Now, I don't want anyone to pray for me, they don't know what I am suffering from, and it is definitely, definitely harmful for all these praying people to mumble off their prayers without having the slightest idea of what they are doing.

Let's mention something which is capable of concrete expression, something which can be used as an example. Prayer is most often useless except in the negative sense and so cannot be demonstrated. Hypnotism can.

Let's say that we have a girl suffering from some complaint. Well-meaning friends insist that she go to a hypnotist. Now, being a bit weak, she goes to this hypnotist. The man may be very well-meaning indeed, he may be carved of solid gold with jewelled insets, but no matter how well-meaning he is unless he is a qualified medical man he doesn't know about the girl's illness and so, although without any doubt whatever he can DISGUISE the symptoms from which the girl is suffering, he cannot cure her, and if he disguises the symptoms or conceals them so that a qualified doctor cannot find the symptoms then the girl might become worse and die adding a load to the hypnotist's kharma and to the stupid "friends" who sent the girl to the hypnotist.

As I know only too well, if one goes to a hospital in acute agony the medical staff there will not give one a drug to relieve one of the pain UNTIL THEY HAVE STUDIED ALL THE SYMPTOMS. Only when they have become acquainted with all the symptoms will they do anything about relieving the pain. Obviously the symptoms are the things which tell the doctors what the patient suffers from. So when we get people praying their heads off they might by some accident of telepathy cause a sort of hypnotic effect and induce a suppression of some vital symptom. I always look on these people who want to pray for me as my greatest enemies, I always say, "God protect me from my friends—my enemies I can deal with." So—no more prayers, no more prayers unless you are definitely and positively asked by the sufferer to pray. If the victim asks for the prayers then that lets you off the hook, but until then—pray for yourself, you probably need it as much as anyone!

Someone wrote to me and took me to task saying that I couldn't have any friends at all, saying that no one could possibly like me because I only mention people who write rudely. As a matter of fact she was a Women's Libber—the lowest form of human existence so far as I am concerned—so perhaps it might be a good thing to tell you now about some of my friends. Some wrote to me, others such as Hy Mendelson who I'll tell you about later—in that case I wrote to him!

It has its problems, I suppose, writing about my friends because if I mention them just as they come into my mind that stupid Women's Lib person who writes so often (always full of hate) will say that I am mentioning men before women or something, so I think I'll mention just a few of my friends alphabetically. In that way surely no one could be offended.

For the benefit of some people I will say now that I will not give the address of any of these people that I

42

mention. Now, just a week or so ago I received an un-stamped letter from a man who said, "State names and addresses of people who can do astral travel so that I can check up on you." The poor fellow was so much of a bum that not only did he omit putting a stamp on the letter, he didn't sign it and didn't put an address either, so I hope he reads this and can appreciate my explanation that I never, never give the names and addresses of other people without first receiving their written permission. I have had a lot of trouble with people getting in touch with me asking about others and I am always irate on such occasions and give the rudest rejoinder that I can think of. So—I give certain names of certain friends, not all my friends because I am not compiling a telephone directory, but just certain people who spring quickly to mind. But under no circumstances will I give their ad-dresses.

Yesterday we had a visitor, one whom we were expect-ing—"we" is Mrs. Rampa, Mrs. Rouse, Miss Cleopatra Rampa and Miss Tadalinka Rampa as well as myself. Soon a great big station wagon rolled up and out came John Bigras. We have known him quite a time. We knew him first when we were at Habitat in the City of Mon-treal. Biggs, as we call him, encountered me there, or would it be more correct to say that I encountered him? Anyway, we liked each other and we have kept a very close association ever since. Biggs used to be a top-flight salesman for medical products. He got some sort of Award on two or three occasions for selling so many goods. But then when we left Montreal he came to the conclusion that there wasn't much future for him in Mon-treal so he followed us all the way across Canada driving a mobile home thing with himself and his two cats; Way-farer, the gentleman cat, is a most immense creature and extremely kind-hearted. His wife-cat is a gentle creature who is about half the size of Wayfarer.

They all settled very comfortably in Vancouver where Biggs has a job, a job that he likes, a job that affords him plenty of movement, plenty of travel, and a chance to meet people. And his cats "keep house."

Yesterday, then, Biggs and two cats came here to Calgary and they are staying near us for about a week while they have a vacation. Biggs thinks Calgary is a nice place but, of course, it is very small compared to Vancouver. Never mind, diamonds are small things, aren't they? And lumps of coal are not! Biggs, then, could be classed as one of our closest friends because we see most of him and we are in contact two or three times a week by telephone.

There are two ladies who were among the very first to write to me when "The Third Eye" came out. One of them is Mrs. Cuthbert, so I can say—good gracious me!—I must have known Mrs. Cuthbert about 17 years. We correspond quite frequently, but I have never met her. So another of my friends, then, is Mrs. Cuthbert, and I will mention the other lady later alphabetically. I have to remember that Women's Libber who is my bête noire.

Now we come to a real rough diamond, a man we all like very much. Frogs Frenneaux. The Frogs bit is because he is an Englishman descended (ascended would sound better) from an old French-origin family. He is always addressed here as Frogs, anyway. Now he lives in New Brunswick. We met him when we lived there also. He is a fine Engineer and although he sometimes speaks quite roughly, growling like a bulldog or worse, he still has a heart of gold. Mind you, now that I have written down "heart of gold" I wonder how a heart of such a metal could work in a human body. Never mind, metaphorically speaking "heart of gold" stands for Frogs Frenneaux. I remember when I was staying at a hotel in Saint John, New Brunswick, Frogs drove me there and he heaved and he hoved and he puffed and he roared, and he pulled my wheelchair backwards up a flight of steps. It nearly killed him, mind, and it even more nearly killed me, but we got up that flight of steps with poor old Frogs looking like a frog should look when he is all puffed up. So let me say, "Hi to you, Frogs."

Hey, I'm still on the Canadian continent, so let me mention another one. My good friend Bernard Gobeille. Oh yes, we know Bernard very well, he is a very nice man indeed. He used to be, in a manner of speaking, my landlord because when I was living at Habitat he was the Man in Charge, he looked after things, and he looked after things very well indeed, in fact he looked after things too well because he was so efficient as an Administrator that he got moved from Habitat and sent as a sort of trouble-shooter to another big apartment complex where they were having troubles. Habitat wasn't the same with Bernard Gobeille missing, and so as I was having trouble with the press as usual that proved to be the last straw, and off my family and I went far from those haunts of Habitat. But Bernard Gobeille and I keep in touch, in fact I had a letter from him this morning. I wish he was here, I wish he was my landlord now, but Calgary is a long way from Montreal.

But why don't we take a trip? Let's go further than Canada, let's go to . . . Brasil for a change. In Brasil there is a most eminent gentleman, Mr. Adonai Grassi, a very good friend indeed. He is learning English especially so that we can correspond without the intervention of a third person. Adonai Grassi is a man with unusual talents, a man with drive and compassion. He is not one of

45

those ruthless dictator type people, he is a man well worth knowing, one of the best type of man, and I predict that he will make his name known thoroughly in Brasil and elsewhere. So how can I send my "saludos" in Portuguese? But he knows what I think of him, and I do think a lot of him.

Shall we go a bit further to greet a gentleman from Mexico, Mr. Rosendo Garcia? Agreed, he is now living in Detroit, U.S.A., but he is still a Mexican, definitely one of the best type of Mexicans, a gentle, educated man who "wouldn't hurt a fly". A gentleman of the world who has had many many hardships definitely not of his making, one whom we could say with absolute truth is on his last life. Next time he will indeed go to a much, much better Round of Existence.

Back again we go to greet my friend Mr. Friedrich Kosin in Brasil. He is a friend of Adonai Grassi. Unfortunately I wrote quite a lot about Mr. Kosin but he sent me letters and a cable protesting at what I said about him. He is too modest or something like that. Frankly I don't know what it's all about, but I will just say that he is a man closely associated with Mr. Grassi.

Now . . . back to a real old stager, my dear old friend, Pat Loftus, who I met—oh—so many years ago. Mr. Loftus is a gentleman of nature, one of the finest men one could meet. He is retired now, but he used to be an Irish policeman, one of the "Gardias", and as a policeman he had a most enviable reputation as a kind man but a stern one too.

I admire Mr. Loftus very much indeed. We have kept closely in touch and if I could have a wish granted that wish would be that I could see him again before either of us leaves this world. We are not so young now, either of us, and there's not much time left, so I fear that this will be a wish unfulfilled.

Mr. Loftus was one of that gallant band of men who founded the Republic of Eire, he was one of the heroes of those early days but he was not favoured by chance, by fortune, as so many of the others were. If fortune had smiled a little Pat Loftus would have been at the head of State in Ireland instead of a retired policeman.

Yes, Mr. Loftus is one of my oldest friends, one of my most esteemed friends, and I am sure that living beside the Irish Sea he often looks out—as he tells me—and thinks of me three thousand miles away. Well, Pat Loftus, I think of you my friend—I think of you.

But we've got to come back to Canada thinking of Mr. Loftus and the way he sits beside the sea looking out towards Canada, and that reminds me of Shelagh McMorran. She is one of the people who wrote to me and has been writing to me ever since. She is one of those whom I have met and—yes, she is a friend. She is a woman of many abilities, many talents, a most capable woman and one whom anyone could like.

A bit further on your journey again (my friends do seem diversified, don't they?), and let's get back to Montreal again and discuss a very particular friend, Hy Mendelson, whom I have referred to as being the most honest man in Montreal. Yes, and I certainly believe it. Some time ago when I was in New Brunswick I wanted a used camera. My wife was idly flicking over the pages of the evening newspaper and she said, "Well, why not write here, Simon's Camera, Craig Street West, Montreal?" So I was a bit slow on the uptake but eventually I did write to Simon's Camera, and I received a very satisfactory reply from—Hy Mendelson. He treated me as an honest man, no cash in advance business with him, no waiting until the cheque was cleared or anything like that. He treated me as I like to be treated, and not only have I dealt with him since but we have built up quite a warm friendship and I hope he likes me as much as I like him.

He has had quite a difficult life, taking over the business from his father and building it up until now I am absolutely positive that he has a bigger stock, a more diversified stock, than any other photographic store in Canada. Sometimes, just for amusement, I have asked him if he has such-and-such a thing in stock and always the answer has been, "Yes!" So, Mr. Hy Mendelson, it's a pleasure knowing you my friend, and you have a distinction in that I wrote to you, you did not write to me.

Shall we have another "M"? Okay, let's move across the border to the U.S.A. and say hello to Mr. Carl Moffet. Because of his interests I have "christened" him Paddle Boat Moffet. He makes models, superbly accurate models, ship models, of course. But as I told him there's no point in making silly old galleons and ancient ships that go along by the wind, he ought to make paddle boats, and so he is doing just that.

Some months ago he made a beautiful model paddle boat and sent me some photographs of it, but then he sent the paddle boat as a gift and, do you know, our customs people here in Calgary wanted to charge such a fantastic price on it that I couldn't afford and nor could Paddle Boat Moffet. And so I was deprived of one of the few pleasures left to me; I was deprived of having this model which had been made so lovingly for me by a very good friend—Paddle Boat Moffet—in the U.S.A. The model had to go back because the customs people wanted hundreds of dollars in customs duty on a hand-made thing, and they were most unreasonable about it.

Still, it's only what one can expect from customs people; I have never got on with them at all.

This time we are going to do some ocean hopping. We are not going to stay on the North American continent, although, of course, we've got to come back. We are going, instead, to Japan, Tokyo. Here lives a very good friend of mine, one who first wrote to me and then who came to see me all the way from Japan, Kathleen Murata. She is small, highly talented, but doesn't appreciate her own abilities. If she could only realize those abilities she could succeed at book illustrating, etc., because, as I say, she is enormously talented.

Kathleen Murata is an American woman married to a gentleman of Japan. I think she suffers greatly from homesickness, I think she wants to get back to the U.S.A. even though that country is just about flooded as an aftermath of Watergate. But she wrote to me, I suppose, in the hope of getting someone to correspond with her as a link within the North American continent, and we have established a very firm friendship. She came to see us when we were at Habitat, Montreal, and she stayed with us for a time in our apartment. We like her a lot.

But—back again to Canada. This time to one of Canada's islands where live Mr. and Mrs. Orlowski—Ed and Pat Orlowski. They are talented, too. Ed is a most skilful craftsman, he can do modelling, he can do all manner of artistic things, but he has never had a chance in life.

He came from old Europe and, I suppose, settled in Canada, and he brought many of the old European skills with him. But I suppose he is on his last life on this Earth, and as such is getting more than his share of hardships. He has a very poor job, very very poorly paid, and yet, I tell you truly, the man is a genius. All he needs is an opportunity, all he needs is a bit of financing so he can make his statuettes, his figurines. At present I have given him some designs so he can make Pendulums, Touch Stones, and Eastern type pendants, things at which he excels. Yes, I'll tell you what I'll do; I'll give you his address, I'll break my rule, so that if you want to order some wonderful articles you can write to Ed Orlowski and find out what he's got available. All right, then, here is his address:—

> Mr. Ed Orlowski,
> Covehead,
> York P.O.,
> Prince Edward Island,
> Canada.

Not too far away from that place is a very good American, Captain George "Bud" Phillips, a most admired friend of mine, a man who goes racing around the continent in a Lear Jet. He is Senior Pilot for a very big firm and he certainly sees life, usually from above 30,000 feet! I know Captain Phillips quite well, and the more I get to know him the more I get to admire his sterling qualities.

Let's move a bit "to the right" and then we can call in on Mrs. Maria Pien. She is a Swiss woman married to a Chinese—I'd better say Chinese man or our Women's Libber will write and ask how a woman can marry a woman, although I understand they do nowadays, in fact I read something about it recently. Anyway, Maria Pien is a woman with such a lot of abilities but unfortunately she has a family and the family takes up a lot of her time. And when you have a family taking up time then you have to put aside your own inclinations, don't you, and get on and look after your responsibilities. So, hello Maria, glad to mention you as a friend of mine.

Another one, this time a man, Brian Rusch. He is an old correspondent of mine too. We have been writing to each other for—oh, I wouldn't like to say how long, to be quite honest I can't remember how long it's such a time ago. But he is one of my earliest correspondents.

Ruby Simmons is another. She is the one who wrote to me—well, I think she wrote to me, actually, before Mrs. Cuthbert did. As far as I remember now Ruby Simmons was actually the first correspondent in the U.S.A., and we write regularly, and that is why she is listed here as one of my friends.

Away in Vancouver there is a lady who attracted me very much because of her interest in Bonsai, that, you know, is Japanese dwarf trees. Mrs. Edith Tearo knows a lot about gardens and plants and all that, and we have made quite a friendship because of our mutual interest in dwarf trees. As a matter of interest she came to see me the weekend before last. Of all curious things she got in her car on a Friday evening and drove 670 miles or so from Vancouver to Calgary. She stayed at my house a very short time indeed, and then hopped back into her car and drove all the way home to Vancouver so she would be ready for work at the start of the week. Now, isn't that a good friend for you? One who will get in a car and drive 670 miles twice? Well, I suppose she got a breath of fresh air doing it, but anyway she was certainly welcome here.

Move on again across another ocean to Eric Tetley in England. He wrote to me some time ago and I was quite amused by his name, it reminded me of Tetley teabags which we use here, so of course I replied to him and in my usual tactless way reminded him about Tetley teabags. Since that time quite a friendship has ripened between us. We like each other, we write to each other, we exchange naughty jokes at times. Of course we have to be careful, we can't say our best jokes to either one of us because—well, you know what it is when there are ladies in the house, they will read a letter sometimes and they wouldn't like a mere male to see that they couldn't blush after all. Anyway, Eric Tetley and I are good friends by correspondence.

Jim Thompson is another good friend. He lives in the wilds of California. I always thought that all California was wild, especially as I have been there a few times. My! They are a wild lot there, aren't they? I'd better not tell you how many of the people I have mentioned above come from California!

But Jim Thompson and I have been corresponding for a terrific time, we've got to know each other very thoroughly, and there is one peculiarity about Jim Thompson which I just must share with you; he seems to have cornered the world market in calendar pages going back to 1960, and invariably he writes to me on a calendar page dated 1960. I didn't know there were so many old calendars left in the world. Anyway, Jim Thompson and I are quite good friends.

Glory be, do you know I have given twenty people already? Twenty, think of that. Still, some of you have asked about my friends so now you are getting some information about a few of them. I think we will mention just one more because this is a friend in Belgium—Miss L. C. Vanderpoorten. She is a very important lady indeed with many business interests and we write to each other not too often but enough to ensure that there is a good friendship. She is such a busy woman with her business interests that I think she hasn't too much time for private correspondence. I know just how she feels! I want, then to say hello to Miss Vanderpoorten away in far off Belgium.

Well, those of you who have asked me about my friends and have impolitely intimated that I couldn't have any friends, you might be a little surprised, eh? Mind you, I know I have left out a lot of people in this small reference but if I added any more I am sure my publisher would have something to say!

Hey though, Mr. Publisher, I've got you after all! You said you wanted a book answering Readers' questions. Well, Honourable Sir, that's what I am doing; a lady Libber (sorry, no Women's Libber can be a lady by their own admission) asked me if I didn't have any friends; and if I had, to list them on the back of a postage stamp. It would have to be a big postage stamp, wouldn't it? But I have given just a few, so I haven't broken any rules, Mr. Publisher. I am answering Readers' questions!

CHAPTER FOUR

It was a very nice sunny afternoon. Biggs, our guest from Vancouver, said, "Why don't I take you out this afternoon—go anywhere you like?" I thought of all the work to be done, I thought of all the letters to be answered because I had been in hospital and a number of people had been informed of it explaining the delay in answering their letters, so everyone had started writing back asking all manner of questions and then people were asking more and more questions so I would have something to do when I got out of hospital! Yes, I have plenty to do!!

Then there was a book to be written. If I didn't get the typescript finished, the Publisher couldn't give it to the Printer to be set up. Then I thought, "Oh well, it does say somewhere that all work and no play makes Jack a dull boy. I'm a dull boy anyway, so I'll go out."

I trundled onto the car in my wheelchair and, with the usual difficulty, got into the car. The wheelchair was folded up and put in the trunk and off we went.

This was my first trip out of the house since leaving the hospital some time before. Actually it was the first opportunity I had had of seeing anything at all of Calgary because we have no car. We have no television either. Sometimes I believe there are programmes about a city on TV, but I am barred from that also. On this day, then, we took off and headed toward the mountains leaving the city behind us, and went on climbing up the high rise of the foothills. First, though, we took a circuit around the hospital, the Foothills Hospital of Calgary, a very fine, very modern hospital, and the first thing we saw was a body being loaded from the Mortuary into a hearse!

We turned about and continued on over the river up into the rising ground. I could not go too far because now I tire so easily and suffer so much pain, so—we stopped for a time on high ground where we could look over the city, quite a pleasant city it is, too, with the winding rivers—the Bow and the Elbow—threading their way through the city.

The traffic was awful. We are told there are more cars per capita in Calgary than anywhere else in North America and I well believe it. People seem to zoom along without a care in the world. Well, there are quite good hospitals to receive them!

All too soon the time came to return home, so we took a different road through a shopping centre, and I must confess to considerable amazement at the way all the shops nowadays seem to be leaving the centre of cities and going far out on the outskirts, leaving the centre of the cities for—what? Offices? I suppose it must be used for something.

But we can't waste the whole day, the time has come to work, and I am going to be an old crosspatch again because have a pet peeve.

I do indeed hate it when people write to me as though I were a poor benighted heathen urgently needing salvation.

For some extraordinary reason "do-gooders"—holy Joe's and holy Joess's—have been writing to me in increasing numbers of late and sending me all manner of New Testaments, Old Testaments, "good words" and all the rest of it. One woman wrote to me yesterday and said, "I hope the Light of the Dear Lamb, the Lord Jesus, sparks a response in your heart. You can only be saved by the blood of Jesus." Well, fine. By the way she writes—a real vicious old so-and-so she is about heathens —she needs some of that salvation herself. Anyway, I am a Buddhist. I was born a Buddhist, I am a Buddhist, and I shall die a Buddhist. Now, Buddhism is not a religion, it is a Way of Life, and the real Buddhists never try to convert others to their Belief. Now, I understand, there is some sort of cult who call themselves Buddhists who go out like missionaries and yowl in the streets. Well, they are not true Buddhists. We have no missionaries, and I don't want any missionaries preaching to me. I had one of those in the hospital the last time I was in, and I soon convinced him I knew something about Christianity too!

I firmly believe that unless we have a return to religion

55

on this world soon we shall have no world left. But I equally firmly believe that it does not in the least matter what form that religion takes. What does it matter whether one is a Buddhist, a Jew, a Christian, a Hindu, or anything else, so long as we believe in certain things? If we do then we will act in a certain way, and my belief is, "Do unto others as you would have them do unto you." I never try to make converts, and I don't want people to try to convert me. So will you remember that, please, all incipient do-gooders? If I get these books, holy words, holy terrors, holy this and holy that they go straight into the garbage unopened because I find that the type of person who goes to the trouble of sending these things is usually the most ignorant and the most bigoted of all types of people. They are so set in their religion, so hypnotized by it, that they are not able to stand apart and study what really is the origin of a religion.

Some of you seem to have been very greatly interested in the report in my last book, "Candlelight", about Jesus going to Japan and about the report of the brother of Jesus being crucified as a substitute. So perhaps I should do what so many of you have asked me to do—say a bit more about some of the old Bible stories. A surprising number of people have written to me asking—More, more.

Obviously you must keep in mind at all times that there isn't much mention of any of this sort of thing except in the Bible. For example, none of the great writers of round about two thousand years ago wrote anything at all about Christ. That's a thought worth pondering; any event nowadays is written up everywhere in inaccurate detail, and with all the trimmings that the press can devise. But throughout history great writers invariably wrote about events of moment, and the fact that none of the writers of crucifixion days wrote anything at all about crucifixion implies that Jesus wasn't known except to a very few people.

Just remember this; Christianity did not come until long after Christ. Actually the foundations of Christianity were set at the Convention of Constantinople sixty years after the date of the alleged crucifixion. In the opinion of great Greek and Roman writers of the day Jesus was a sort of trouble-maker, one who had certain ideas and at the present day we should say, "Oh, he's just a member of a hippy gang or the leader of a set of robbers."

Shocked? Well, you shouldn't be, you know, because you were not there, you do not know the facts, you only know what has been peddled to you through the Bible and Bible stories. Great writers of the day whose words have survived and reached us now made no mention of Jesus.

Another thing to be considered is this; if a person were to be crucified and then at the end of the day the person was removed from the cross he could be revived, THE CRUCIFIXION DIDN'T KILL HIM! Actually, being suspended by the arms as on the cross there were very serious difficulties and obstacles in the matter of breathing. It was impossible to take a full breath because to take a full breath means to expand the chest, and when one is suspended by one's arms that cannot be done. I have been so suspended in a prisoner-of-war camp so I can speak from experience. So the crucifixion wouldn't kill. Instead there would be extreme exhaustion and soon the person would sink into a coma during which his breathing would become very very shallow, growing shallower, so eventually you could say that he died of suffocation.

I understand much the same sort of thing occurs when a person is electrocuted. The muscles controlling breathing are paralysed or impaired, and so there is not enough air taken in to make available to the brain the necessary oxygen with which to sustain consciousness. So in that case a person lapses into unconsciousness, and IF NEGLECTED the person would eventually die. If he could be removed from the source of electricity and artificial respiration given he would in most cases revive.

I was going to tell you some very interesting things— true things—about certain aspects of prison life in the U.S.A., but for some reason my publisher seems to think what I originally wrote would cause great alarm to American readers. In deference to my publisher I have to leave out certain parts, but I will suggest you get hold of a book or two written by former prison Governors in the U.S.A. Some of these men have written very revealing books about certain aspects of prison life in the U.S.A., and although my publisher will not let me mention these facts, the American publishers of the prison Governors' books are not so nervous. So—go along to your Public Library and see if you can find some titles of books by prison Governors in the U.S.A.

Do you know that in bygone days there was a definite law that when a person was crucified the body should be removed at nightfall? Before removal from the cross the legs had to be broken so as to give the body an extra shock and an extra strain on the chest, and thus upon the breathing muscles. But let me remind you that in the case of Jesus it was specifically stated that His bones were not broken. So if His bones were not broken and if He did not get that extra shock, then possibly the body could have been revived.

As I have said above, in the case of Jesus the body was

removed without the legs having been broken and the body—no one has said it was a dead body, remember—was hustled away to a cave and there it was received by a very special, very gifted, band of men and women.

You have heard of the Essenes, you have heard that they were a very special band of most knowledgeable people who had training and skills beyond the understanding of the average person in the street.

They had an extraordinarily high knowledge of life and death, they knew what chemicals to use, they knew how to revive bodies. So in the cave very quickly pungent aromatics were administered to the crucified person, and chemicals were injected, and eventually the body—whether it be Jesus or the brother of Jesus or someone else, it doesn't matter—was revived.

To refresh your mind a little further remember the case of Lazarus. Lazarus was reportedly revived from the dead, wasn't he? Now, there is that definite report. There is the report, also, that Jesus revived him. Jesus was a member of the Essenes, so it is very likely that Jesus, a "White Magician", had certain herbs or powers with which He could accomplish these seeming miracles, and such a miracle was worked upon Lazarus who may have been in a coma. After all, there is a possibility that it could even have been a diabetic coma. Let me tell you something; I am diabetic, I have been in diabetic comas, and in such a state in certain conditions one can easily be taken for dead.

Another type of complaint which simulates death is the complaint of catalepsy. Many people suffering from that have actually been buried—buried alive—because the true cataleptic can undergo all tests except one; he has no responses, no reflexes, and a mirror held to his lips will not fog. There is only one test infallible in the case of the

59

cataleptic—the test of decay. If a body dies it starts to decay, and after a certain time one's eyes and one's nose give complete assurance that the body is indeed dead, but that does not happen in the case of a cataleptic. So possibly Lazarus was in a coma or cataleptic state and Jesus, as a member of the Essenes, realized the condition and had the ability to treat it. If we do not know the technique of a thing then it becomes a miracle, doesn't it, particularly if, according to our own concept, it is against established law or belief or knowledge.

Well, just remember that there are a certain number of books in the Bible, but there were many many more books which had to be omitted from inclusion in "the Bible." The Bible, of course, is just a collection of books as the word implies.

Many other "gospels" had to be left out because they contradicted the testimony of the few who were published. Think of this; it is nowhere said that the Bible is true. Instead you have a statement "The Gospels ACCORDING to St. Somebody." In other words, we are getting fair warning that this is not necessarily a true book, instead it is a book which has been reported ACCORDING to the words of a certain person. It is much the same as saying, "Well, he told me that he thought . . ." That is not saying that you know it for a fact. Instead, according to the language of the lawyers, it could be classified as hearsay evidence, not something which is given to you as utter truth, incontrovertible truth, but as a statement according to someone else.

If you could get hold of other old books, papyrii, or stone writings, you would find that there were truly remarkable divergencies. Do you know, some books say that John never lived? Some people say that John was just a symbolical, a mythical, figure like John Bull in

England or G.I. Joe in the U.S.A., or—what is it?—Kilroy Was Here.

If you would do astral travel as I suggest you shouldn't have much difficulty in finding out these things for yourself because there are still quite a number of documents going back two or three thousand years or even longer which have not been discovered by physical Man. But Man in the astral—and Woman in the astral, too—can find these things and can read them. There is a great advantage because many of these papyrii are stuck together with age, and if you tried to unroll them now in the physical they might shatter into dust, but in the astral you can go through them layer by layer without disturbing their physical structure.

If you find that difficult to understand get hold of a microscope somewhere and look at, let us say, a piece of rough stone. You can carefully focus your microscope and you can see different layers of the stone coming into focus, being quite clear, and then disappear to provide space for another focus. Anyone with a microscope can explain that to you.

My wife has just read this and she has made a worthwhile suggestion. She said, "Why not tell them that some people believe that Sherlock Holmes was a living person?" Well, that's a good point, a very good point, because Sherlock Holmes has been accepted as a living person and people still write to him. I suppose the letters go to the estate of Conan Doyle, but Sherlock Holmes was a figment of the imagination of Conan Doyle. We know there was no such entity as Sherlock Holmes, but popular imagination has clothed that imaginary entity with an existence, in fact in England there is, I believe, a Club devoted to perpetuating the legend or myth of Sherlock Holmes.

Well, I have mentioned using astral travel to get to see some of the undiscovered manuscripts, etc. During the past twenty years I have had an enormous number of people write and tell me that now they can do astral travel, they can experience the reality of what I have been writing about. They tell me that after the first initial struggle they felt that they had "broken free" and they could travel at will anywhere at any time.

Unfortunately a number of people have written to me calling me a fake, etc., and saying all manner of things, which I am sure they will regret, because they personally could not do astral travel. And I can only assume that if a person has the wrong attitude—if a person makes the wrong approach—and has doubts or fears, then it's not so easy to do astral travel. To me and to thousands and thousands more there is no problem, or rather, the only problem is how to tell others how easy it is.

Let's have a look at this astral travel thing again, shall we. You want to do astral travel; first of all, do you believe in astral travel? Are you convinced that there is such a thing as astral travel which you can do given such-and-such conditions? If your answer is "No" then go no further because you will not be able to astral travel unless you are thoroughly convinced of its existence. You have to convince your sub-conscious because to my way of thinking the sub-conscious and the astral body are something like a boy holding a helium-filled balloon; as long as the boy holds on to the balloon it is quite literally attached to his body, but if the boy can be induced to let go the string then the balloon will float upwards. The astral travel condition is like that. So—first of all you must believe that astral travel is possible. Secondly you must believe that you can do astral travel.

When astral travelling it is quite impossible for any

entity or anything to cause you harm unless you are afraid. Now, if you think that is strange just think of this; if you sit back comfortably in a chair and you think of some imaginary ailment, and you think of all the pain and distress that such an ailment could cause, you then think that you may have it so your heart starts to palpitate and you might feel a bit upset. Then you are sure you have something wrong with you and your heart races even more, and soon, because of your heart racing, you will get a gastric condition, you will feel bilious or something else. So it's quite possible for you to make yourself definitely ill if you believe you have some illness which is perhaps incurable. In the same way, if you try to do astral travel feeling sure that some bogey is going to jump out and pull your tail feathers or something, then you will be afraid to do astral travel and, in that case, it is a waste of time trying. So a third condition is that you must have no fear of astral travel. Fear will definitely prevent you from getting out of the body.

Assuming, though, that you are convinced of the truth of astral travel, and assuming that you are convinced that you want to do it, and being certain that you have no fear, then really there shouldn't be any obstacle unless you want to astral travel for a bad purpose. For example —and this is true—I have had men of a sort write to me telling me they wanted to astral travel so they could see girls undressing and so on. I had one man write to me and tell me that he wanted to astral travel so that he could be sure his girl was a virgin before he married her! That, I assure you, is absolutely true, and it is a good way to make sure you don't astral travel at all.

But assuming that you are able to satisfy the conditions, you believe in astral travel, you believe that you, given a bit of help, could travel easily, you have no fear and you have no intention of using the ability for anything wrong, then—you should sit down somewhere where it's not too light and not too dark, it must be just neutral. Sit down so that you are completely comfortable, so comfortable that you are not aware that you are sitting down or lying down, and there are no sharp edges sticking into you. And then you definitely visualize yourself getting out of the body. Breathe regularly, make deep and rhythmic breaths, and then let your eyes (which are closed) roll up so that you are, in effect, gazing at a spot somewhere near your hairline—if you are bald you have to imagine where your hairline would be!

Your eyes, then, should be squinting to a slight extent so that their focus converges, as I have said, about the hairline. Just take things easy, there's no point in rushing things, no point at all, let things go at their own speed. Then either one of three things will happen. You might suddenly find that you have made a jerk. If you jerk then you might come back straight into the body because it means that you got out of the body and then took fright. The fright will have sent you right back in again. There is nothing to be worried about in that. You can, if you like, sigh with exasperation and start all over again.

The second thing that can happen to you is that you might feel a very very slight—well, I can only say numbness—which might start at the feet and spread upwards. It isn't quite a numbness, really it is indescribable unless you have actually had it happen to you. It could be numb, it could be a slight tingling. But, anyway, it is something different, and you have to try to ignore it. It is perfectly normal, anyway. Some people after this find that they are almost in a cataleptic state, their muscles tighten up, they will not be able to move. Well—be careful, whatever you do don't panic here—that is a very very good sign because you have your eyes shut, remember, and yet here at this stage you will find that you are able to "see" through your eyelids, but everything will have a golden tinge. And then, when you have reached that stage, you will find a swaying sensation and out you will go straight into the astral and you will see things brighter and more vivid and with a greater range of colours than you ever thought possible.

In the third condition, when you have rested you will find, possibly, a swaying. You will experience a sensation that you are going through a tunnel toward a light at the far end of the tunnel. You will be drifting upwards like a piece of thistledown on an evening breeze. Keep calm, that's all to the good because soon you will find the light is growing larger and larger, and then you will drift out of this tunnel and find yourself in a far greater light, you will find that you are actually in the astral world. The grass about will be greener, far greener than you ever thought possible. And the waters about, perhaps a lake or a river, will be so clear that you will be able to see the bottom. It's a wonderful feeling, a wonderful sensation, and if you think of going to a certain place there will be a sort of "blink" and you will be at that place. Suppose, for instance, you've got out into the astral and for a time you float a few inches above the ground just looking about you, marvelling at the conditions, wondering what to do next. You may want to explore in the astral world where everything is brilliant, where the colours are brighter, where there is a tingling sparkle in the air. Well, do so. It certainly will revitalize you. It will build up your psychic powers enormously. It is far better to do this and have some "spiritual feeding". If you do that you will find you will have no difficulty whatever in getting into the astral on any other occasion, but if you want to rush off somewhere for some materialistic purpose then you will find a few shocks.

Suppose you want to go and see XY to see what he is doing; immediately you think of him and think of his location you get there, but you have left the brilliant surroundings and the healthy atmosphere of the astral world, instead you are back on Earth again—in the astral state, admitted—still seeing things as people see them on Earth, dull colours, dull people, muddy water, and if your friend, XY, is in a commercial mood you will find that his colours are pretty dim too, and you won't like it a bit.

My definite recommendation is that those who get into the astral world should stay in that world for perhaps half an hour to get accustomed to it, because then they will find it so very much easier to get into the astral on other occasions.

The big difficulty is with most people that they start off very well indeed, they start getting into the astral, and then their body creaks, they feel strange tugs and sway-ings, sometimes they get almost airsick because they are in such a state of nerves. Well, they get out of the body and then they panic, "Oh, what if I can't get back in again?" Immediately they have the thought—BONK!—and they are back in the body feeling, perhaps, a bit dizzy. And if you do ever get back into the body like that and you feel sick and dizzy, then make sure you lie very still and try to have a sleep, even though it be of only a few minutes, because until your astral body can get out of your physical body and realign itself and so enter cor-rectly, you will have quite a bit of indisposition. So—no amount of aspirins will help you, all you need is to get out of your body again and back in properly. It's like getting up in the morning and finding you've got the wrong shoe on the wrong foot, you wouldn't want to go about all day like that so you change your shoes to the right feet. In the same way, get out of your body again and back in properly.

So that's all there is to it. I say that anyone who can comply with the conditions can do astral travel—anyone at all. But if you are afraid or if you are doubtful then don't waste time because you won't astral travel.

Let me return to the original theme of this Chapter; religion. I have said a few things about the Christian religion and about the various fighting factions of that religion. I have said that I have no religion as Buddhism is not a religion, it is a Belief instead. All right, what do I think of Buddhism?

The more one studies Buddhism the more one can appreciate the intrinsic value of it AS A GUIDE TO LIVING, and the more one can realize that Gautama was negative in his outlook.

My personal Belief, which I have never put in print before, is that Gautama, the Prince, was too utterly sheltered from the hard facts of life, and then when he suddenly became confronted with suffering, pain and death, then it "turned his brain," it gave him a severe psychic shock, it upset his sense of values, it destroyed something essential to his being. So the Prince Gautama left the Palace, left all the comforts he had known, and became utterly disillusioned. My personal Belief is that he became "negative."

If one studies the Teachings of Gautama (let us say "Buddha" which is more normal to Western people) one will appreciate that Buddha was negative, everything was "no-ness," "all life is suffering." Well, we know that isn't true, don't we? There are good times in life as well as bad times. So I believe that Buddha became far too

67

negative in his outlook, but at the same time he did produce for the world some very very valuable precepts, and it was founded on the much older religion of Hinduism. So we have Hinduism as one of the older religions, and Buddha took valuable portions of the Hindu belief and formulated what was called Buddhism, in the same way that Christ did not wander in the Wilderness at all, instead He travelled through India and into Tibet studying all the time and being taught all the time the Higher Teachings of Hinduism, Buddhism, the Islamic belief, and others, and from that He formulated that which became known in distorted form as Christianity. Again we must be sure that we realize that the "Christianity" of Christ was not the very altered version which was propagated in the year 60 to increase the power of the priests. Now, I have been forbidden to mention anything about these priests in this particular book, but I have already written about them in many of my books. Just for one illustration, to see what I am trying to get over to you—but because of the new conditions must not say outright—please read "The Hermit", page 154. I still do not understand how a publisher who has published these things can now decide that they must not be published. It seems a question of double talk to me, but I am supposed to be—I have been told—too out-spoken. Anyway, I am not mealy-mouthed, am I!?

Well, to get back to our bit about religion, these priests of the early days, because of their own peculiar—ah—"naughty-naughty" outlook on life (I hope no one is blushing?) taught that women were evil and everything about women was unclean, which, of course, is not the modern view at all. If you want to know the modern view just read about the Women's Lib, and then you'll think that if women think that way then possibly they are unclean!

My own personal belief is that the only salvation available to the world at the present time is in a form of religion, it doesn't matter what sort of religion, any religion will do provided you really believe it. You have your belief, I will have mine, and if we are both people of good intention then it will not matter that possibly some of the terms we use are different. The world now is a very dissolute place. Instead of being disciplined young people do not respect age any more, children do not respect their parents. So if we make a religion which teaches such respect then we are several steps ahead of the rest, aren't we?

There must be a return to religion before the world can be set right, but one of the greatest things in religion is that we treat others as we would wish to be treated ourselves. That means we've got to share, we've got to give because, quite truly, it is far better to give than to receive, it certainly makes you feel better if you find that you have really helped some person. So—if we would all live as we think that other people should live instead of being a bit hellish ourselves and condemning anyone else who even looks the wrong way or is the wrong colour, then we would be doing something.

I try, as far as I am able, to live according to my own Belief, and as I look back through the days and weeks and months and years of quite a long life I see many things that I could have done better. But never mind, I've got to the stage now where I can do nothing more about it. Although I get bad tempered at times—plenty of you tell me so, anyway!—I still try to live according to my own Belief which is Do Unto Others As You Would Have Others Do Unto You.

There is another little saying well known in the Far East which also applies in living a better life. It is: "Let not the Sun go down upon your wrath." In other words, if you are having a fight with anyone make sure you knock him out and jump on him before darkness falls! Otherwise if you astral travel he may come along and give an astral bonk on some part of your anatomy.

Seriously, though, you should never end a day on a note of anger because it colours your reactions in the astral world, and it really does play havoc with your gastric secretions!

Well, I can now cease my role as a preacher and so I will dismount, complete with wheelchair, from my soapbox and say—that's the end of another Chapter, isn't it?

CHAPTER FIVE

"Your covers are terrible—just like the cheapest kind of science fiction," wrote the happy little soul who had to have SOMETHING about which to find fault. Normally I should have chucked his letter straight into the garbage bin and not given it a second thought, but unfortunately I have had such a lot of letters taking me to task for the covers of my books, particularly the cover of "The Third Eye". I am told it is hideous, disgusting, beastly, enough to put anyone off, and all that sort of thing. Well, dear beloved Readers with love in your hearts, and those without any love anywhere, let me tell you this; I am just the author, you know, the poor fellow who writes some words and sends it off to a publisher. Now, I hope that what I write gets published, I hope that sometime I may be able to get some illustrations in a book. In this particular book I wanted illustrations connected with the hollow Earth, etc., but the publisher is the only one who can say what the cover shall be, the author has no say whatever about the cover. In fact, most times the poor fellow doesn't see the cover until some irate reader sends him a copy with a devastatingly offensive letter blaming the author for everything.

I am responsible for the words, but I am not responsible for the covers, nor am I responsible for the lack of illustrations, nor am I responsible for the quality or lack of quality of the paper. If you don't like those things— well, for Pete's sake, get out your pens or your type- writers and you write to the publisher and tell HIM off—not me. This is one time when I am innocent, there aren't many times when I'm innocent but this time—yes!

Another thing people complain to me about is what they claim is the high price of my books. Some people say the price is excessive. Well, I disagree emphatically. When people write to me complaining about the price of my books I remind them that they will go to a cinema or theatre, or go out drinking their heads off, or they will spend money on cigarettes, and not complain at all about it, and yet for the price they pay for my books they can have a completely new outlook on life—or on death. So take it from me, I think the price of my books is ex- tremely reasonable, and I wish the publisher would double that price!

Now Gail Jordan writes to me and asks me some ques- tions. One question is—"Is it wrong for a woman to cut her hair? Does it interfere with her aura or her spiritual vibration in any way?"

No, of course not. Hair is just a bit of growth which

really doesn't matter at all. All this stuff about Samson being weak as a result of having his hair cut is a mistranslation. What happened was the poor fellow was beguiled too much by Delilah and he got too energetic sexwise and that really weakened him!

So, ladies, cut your hair if you want to, shave the whole darn lot off if you want to. In fact, when you become a Women's Libber you will probably have to shave the whole lot off and glue it on your chin to show you are the equal to a man and that you have a beard.

Question Two from the same person is that I mentioned in one of my books that a man and woman could be compatible if their vibrations were on the same level. How does a man and a woman reach the same level of vibration?

Well, by having the same sort of nature. It's not like tuning a piano. You have to make sure that these two people like each other, that they can put up with the undoubted faults of the other. There is no other way to do it. If they like the same type of reading, the same type of music, the same type of entertainment—well then, undoubtedly their vibrations will be much the same.

It is not possible to know when you are marrying the right partner, but nowadays marriage seems to be a very haphazard business. I know a young couple who have been living together without marriage for four years, they got on quite well together. Then they got married, and they have been knocking each other's head off ever since. Again, near where I live, there is a young woman who is now in a state of hating everyone because she got married and after a week or two found that marriage was not what she expected so without giving marriage a chance she rushed off and got a divorce. Now she is a bitter, frustrated woman and certainly looks it.

Marriage is a very important business, and like all important businesses it should not be entered into lightly. There is a lot of give and take in marriage, and nowadays women are such spoiled babies, such arrant Women's Libbers with their equality stunt that they just do not give marriage a chance to work, and the way things are going on soon there won't be any more marriages. Soon people will just live together for a time and have a baby, and then when the Communist State comes the State will take over the baby's welfare and that's all there will be to it, and so there will be a breakdown of civilization.

Let me tell you something; women nowadays are neurotic, they go off their heads at the drop of a hat because they are trying to compete with men and they are not organically equipped to compete with men in all fields of work. So they get frustrated and they have a mental breakdown. Well, it shows they are a bit loose in the top storey to go in for this Women's Lib stuff, anyway.

In the old days a woman looked after her family, she looked after the children and she was healthy. She was also happy. You don't see happy women nowadays, they are always ready to move the chip on their shoulder and toss it in some man's face.

Another question, "What is your astrological sign?" That I never tell. I think it is an impertinence to ask. If I wanted people to know my astrological sign or my birth data, then I would have told them so in my books. So, I have had a lot of letters from would-be astrologers who were going to set the world alight with their brilliance, who wanted to know my data so they could work out my horoscope for me, but they never get a polite answer from me.

Say—Miss Jordan has a lot of questions; here is the

fourth one, "As a person reincarnates does he follow the signs in order beginning with Aries and ending with Pisces?"

No he doesn't. He comes not merely in the sign but in the quadrant of the sign which will afford him the best opportunity for learning in that life that which he has to learn in that life. He has eventually to live through every sign, and every quadrant of every sign, not, as I said, in the order of the Zodiac. And he may have to live dozens of lives in just one quadrant of one sign because, remember, we live thousands of lives on Earth.

Five, "You stated in one of your books that music could raise one's level of vibration so that one can become more spiritual. Could you list some composers, songs, musical arrangements, etc.?"

No, of course not, because what suits some people does not suit others. I, for example, am very partial to Chinese and Japanese music and some of the Western music really sets my nerves on edge, I don't know why people like it. So if I gave my own list of music the average Westerner would get a pain in his eardrums. So each person has to find the music which is most suitable for him, but I tell you here and now, most most definitely— most emphatically—that people are ruining themselves with this awful "rock" music, and this awful jazz muck. Such music—if one can use such a term for such a con- glomeration of noise—causes nerve strain. Look at some of the young people, the hippies, for instance, who go in for these rock festivals—well, they are a dim looking lot, aren't they? Most of them look as if they are drop-outs from some mental home. Just take a look at them yourself and see what you think.

All right, here's your last question Gail Jordan: "Have you ever heard of the chain letter that has gone around the world a number of times? After a person receives this letter he is supposed to send it to twenty people. Supposedly, according to the letter, if you don't continue the chain death will follow. Anyway, this letter has frightened and upset many people, especially older people. What do you think about it?"

I think that the people who write these chain letters should get their brains tested, always assuming that one can find some brains to test. I have had quite a lot of these ridiculous things sent to me, and if possible I trace the last sender and send back the letter together with a reply which is hoped will singe his eyebrows. I think chain letters are the epitome of crassness. I just don't understand why people place any belief in such arrant nonsense; of course you won't die if you fail to send on these letters. If there had been any truth in it I would have died many many times during the past twenty years. So in my opinion if you get one of these letters try to trace anyone on the list and send it back with an expression of your opinion about the mental stability of the person who sent it. It shakes them; I have had some of them write back to me and apologise and really sincerely thank me. You try it and see!

Now I've got a letter here—I wish it were compulsory to use typewriters because I've got a letter here which is making me go cross-eyed. Anyway, the question is, "You said that the Overself sends down puppets for the purpose of experience. My question is, once an entity experiences the things it was sent down to do does it go back to the Overself and become part of the Overself's mind? Does a person lose his identity as an individual or does he become good friends with his Overself? I personally don't like the idea of just being a part of an entity's mind. I want to remain me. Could you explain this in more detail as I have not found that particular answer in your books."

Well, there is such a lot of confusion about this puppet business; you have to remember that an actor when he is on the stage doing some particular role actually "lives" as that particular identity. But when the show is over and he goes home to his lodgings he can forget all about being Prince Dimwit or someone like that. So the Overself, which cannot be comprehended in the third dimension, is the eventual entity of a human, and the Overself sends down "tentacles" or "puppets" to gather certain information. You might say that you have the head of a detective agency who sits in his office and gathers information by his operatives, those operatives report to him and give him a complete picture of that which he needs to know.

Eventually, after eons of time, all the puppets come together and form the complete entity of the Overself.

Question—"What will happen to people who are involved in Black Witchcraft? As it is a tool for self-gain they must be creating bad kharma. Will they come back as priests, etc.?"

Unfortunately there is a lot of nonsense written about magic, black, white, or any other colour. Most times the black magic person is just living in a fool's paradise. He or she has no power and cannot cast any bad spells, so the only person being harmed is the black magician and he is just being foolish, he is just delaying his evolution. So if a man or woman is a stupid black magician in this life, then that life is deemed to be wasted and the life does not count. So he comes back and starts over where he left on the life before the black magic one.

Of course if the black magician somehow causes harm to another person then it is a black mark added to his kharma and it has to be paid back, but don't wish the poor fellow such a fate that he has to come back as a priest or something because he won't be that important.

Question,—"I have practised my psychic abilities and though I am okay at telepathy I can't seem to acquire the other abilities no matter how hard I try. How can I find my purpose another way? Should I try? Also, how can I find out how many more lives I have on Earth?"

You say you are okay at telepathy but you cannot seem to manage to do the other metaphysical things. Well, I am going to put it to you quite plainly that we are not all gifted in all branches of psychic stuff. Consider just the ordinary, everyday life. As an example you might be able to write, but can you draw? And if you can draw can you write and do sculpture? Most people can do one or two things entirely satisfactorily, but if they are going to excel at all the metaphysical arts then they have to have training starting even before seven years of age, and while I can do everything I write about I have other defects, there are a lot of things I can't do, I can't paint, for instance, I couldn't even paint the wall of a room with whitewash. So we all have our skills, and we all have our lack of skills, and the best thing we can do is to make the most of what we have.

There are certain people we call a genius. Most times such a person is exceedingly brilliant in one line only and in other things he has, more or less, to be led around because all his brain power goes to one specific subject to the detriment of his general knowledge ability.

Question—"People are paying a very large sum of money for Transcendental Meditation. It is a type of meditation that uses neither concentration nor contemplation. It is supposed to just happen when you learn your mantra. I feel that I am more relaxed, etc., but you suggest contemplative meditation. I agree with you as I am a person who thinks about everything. Do you think it is wrong to pay such large sums of money for a course on Transcendental Meditation? My better judgment tells me that somebody is making money out of me and I am being foolish."

Personally I think that people are quite crazy if they want to pay a lot of money for this Transcendental Meditation stuff. I don't even know what it really means. To me it is just a gimmick to get money out of people because you either meditate or you don't meditate, you either walk or you run or you stay still. Now, if you are going to look at a thing are you going to look at it with goose eyes or are you going to look at it sensibly? Let's start a new cult, shall we, and charge a big sum of money. Let's tell people that they can see things better if they look at it with goose eyes. Let's charge them a few hundred dollars. Soon we shall be able to retire and get away from it all.

The Germans, you may remember, used to do a march called the Goose Step. Of course it was very pretty to a distorted mind, but the act of doing the Goose Step was most exhausting for the soldiers. Transcendental Meditation, for which I believe you pay a lot of money, is just, in my opinion, a stupid gimmick. You don't need it. All you need is . . . MEDITATION. That is my honest opinion for which you have asked.

Question—"Can you see a person's aura in a letter or on it? How much can you tell about a person other than the words they write down? I feel really depressed because I don't know why I am here or where I am going or who I am. Can you help me?"

Yes, I can see an aura through a letter. It is by psychometry, though, and that is not so clear as when seeing the actual physical aura. If an aura is to be seen properly and to be of any real use to a person, that person has to be here with me in a room and at least twelve feet from another other person, and the person must be entirely without clothes. Not only that, he or she has to stay without clothes for about half an hour while the effect of the clothes wears off. After all, you wouldn't examine a painting if it was still in its wrappings, would you?

It really does amaze me how difficult it is to obtain women to help in aura research. I understand that there are some remarkable magazines which show "all" and a bit more, some of the illustrations, I am told, are nearly good enough to be used as an anatomical text book. Now, young women, it seems, are most happy to pose definitely in the altogether if they can have themselves photographed and the pictures circulated throughout the world. But when it comes to helping aura research—oh dear, dear, no—they take fright immediately!

I had a woman write to me and say that she was nearly dying with anxiety to help me with aura research. She was quite willing to take off her clothes and stand to be examined or even photographed. She was apparently willing to swear on a stack of Bibles and a stack of Playboy's and Playgirl's too. So, being old and foolish, I saw the woman and—no, nothing would induce her to part with her clothes. She is another of the ones who told me that she had made that offer as a method of getting to see me, but she didn't stay long. It does strike me as truly remarkable that some of these women nowadays will go to bed with any man but they will not take off their clothes for an honest, sincere investigation of the aura. I have had women tell me quite bluntly that they would be delighted to go to bed with me . . . in the dark! Well, I am not interested in that, I live as a monk and I am not interested in the female anatomy except in so far as it will help me with auric research, and that research has come to a standstill for the specific reason that I lack money for equipment and I lack women who will part with their panties!

I have a question here which seems to be a bit remarkable—"Tell me how many more lives I have on Earth."

That seems to be a peculiar question, doesn't it? It is like a person starting school saying, "Tell me when I shall leave school." The answer, of course, depends on such a lot of things. This person who wants to know how many more lives he has—well, what is his state of evolution now? What task is he doing on Earth? How well is he doing that task? Is he trying to help others, or is he interested only in helping himself? Does he intend to go on trying to improve himself, or is he going to engage in all sorts of hellishness? (if a thing can be heavenly, surely it can be hellish as an opposite?)

It is not possible to say how many more lives a person has because the number of lives to be lived depend entirely on the behaviour of the person concerned. It is much like some of these prison sentences being handed out in the U.S.A. nowadays where a person is sentenced to an indeterminate time such as "One to four years." That is, if the person becomes a paragon of virtue in prison and doesn't blot his copybook even once then he can be out in one year, but if he does all the devilment that he can think of he is going to be kept there for the complete four years. So there you are, Mr. So-and-So, the answer to your question is that it all depends on you, on how you behave, so you'd better be good!

Now we've got a gentleman living in South Africa who

has a series of questions which are certainly acceptable for this book. Let's have a look at them, shall we?

"Will the Communists eventually take over this country?"

Yes, in my belief a form of Communism will sweep the world because, you see, nowadays women in particular are trying to get what they call "equality" and they are really gumming up the works. In the old days a man used to go out and earn the money for the living and the woman used to stay at home and look after the family. Nowadays that doesn't happen any more. A woman gets married, goes back to the factory the next day, and eventually, if she is unlucky, she has a baby. She stays home getting full pay, otherwise she shouts, "Discrimination," and then almost as soon as the baby is born it is shoved out with some day nursery people while the mother goes back to the factory. That is all the fault of the capitalists, you know, because their advertising makes people believe they HAVE to have all these wonderful luxuries like at least two cars in every garage, washing machines, TV's, a house in the country, a boat, and all the rest of it. So they rush out and buy these things which they can't afford because they have to "keep up with the Joneses", and then they get their credit cards and they pay interest on those charges. Eventually they are so deeply in debt that they dare not stay away from work. Both husband and wife have to work. Sometimes the husband or the wife has to take double jobs—"moonlighting"—and all the time their indebtedness is increasing.

But worse than that, the offspring are brought up without any parental discipline, without any parental love, and so he or she eventually ends up on the streets lounging about on street corners and falling under the domination of a stronger child who more often than not is evilly inclined. And so we get gangs of hoodlums running about the streets, engaging in vandalism, beating up old people just for the fun of it. I have been reading of a case quite recently where a poor old man, over 65 years of age, was beaten up and robbed by a woman, not only that but she even took his artificial leg!! Now what would a woman want with an artificial leg? Anyway, as long as we have such an undisciplined society we are ripe for Communism. Already we have Socialism. You should go to British Columbia and live under the Government there. I was glad to get away from it! I believe, then, that a modified form of Communism will sweep the world and only when people are willing to live at home and raise a family properly will Communism pass away.

After a much worse time than we have having now—and we are having a bad enough time now, aren't we?—we will have an age when people will slowly awaken from the false values which there are in the world today. Unfortunately people nowadays are hypnotized by advertisements, they believe they simply HAVE to have certain things, they fall prey to subliminal advertising carried out at the cinemas and by television. A person will watch a TV programme and will then after it get up like a person in a dream and stumble out to a car and rush off to some super-market, and come back laden with goods which he or she had no intention of buying and really has no possible use for, all because he or she was unduly influenced by advertising. All that will have to end, and at the risk of appearing to be an old boor I say again that there will have to be a return to some form of religion. People will have to break free of the shackles of selfishness because now they want—want—want—and they don't particularly mind how they get it. We have the age of the "rip-off" wherein young people think it is definitely dishonourable to pay for things, instead they go into stores and ships and they make a definite practise of stealing. They go in numbers and they distract the shopkeeper or clerk, and while that poor wretch is distracted accomplices race through the store and just take anything they want, anything that takes their fancy. I have seen it happen when I was in Vancouver. I sat in Denman Mall, in my wheelchair of course, and I actually watched this happen, and I reported it to a sales clerk who just shrugged her shoulders and said, "But what can I do? I can't run after them or the whole store will be taken while my back is turned." So—there will not be a Golden Age until people have had very very much more suffering, they will have to go through all manner of hardships until their psyche gets such a battering that they cannot take hardships any more and so they awaken from their almost-hypnotized state of being a tool to the advertising people. But even then they won't get much satisfaction out of life until the woman stays at home and forgets her Women's Lib aspirations and raises a family with decency, dignity, and discipline.

There is another question here—"Will the next Master or Spiritual Leader begin his reign before or after the future World War? Surely the intelligent beings that will eventually settle here from afar are more spiritually advanced than one from Earth?"

We cannot have a real "Leader" until people are ready for him. They will have to suffer much more first, and I am going to tell you now that none of these much advertised, much touted "Guru's" are in anyway to be regarded as a World Leader. I have in mind one young man who has made a real packet out of being a "spiritual leader." Apparently he has gone back to India and his own Government—and the income tax authorities!—have caught up with him.

There is a Leader already ready for this Earth, but until conditions are suitable here on Earth he doesn't have a chance, and so he will not make his presence known until the conditions are suitable. After all, what is a hundred years or so, or a thousand years or so, in the lifetime of a world? You see, all this civilization will eventually pass away and others will come, rise up, collapse and pass away to make room for others because this Earth is just a training school, and if we don't make a good job of it now—well, we keep on coming back until we have more sense.

We people who write books get all manner of strange letters, for instance I have had quite a few letters from people who tell me that they are tired of being pushed around, they've seen an advertisement for Karate, or Judo, or any of the Eastern "martial arts," and they are going to rush off and take a course so that—according to them—right after the first lesson they can go out and really toss a bully over their shoulders, and what do I think about it?

I think such people are stupid. To start with, in my firm belief, many of these people who advertise these Karate Courses or other Courses, especially when they are by correspondence, really should be prosecuted because you just cannot teach such things by correspondence. And furthermore, one should never try to learn Karate or Judo, or any of those things, except from an acknowledged and licensed teacher of the art.

Nowadays it seems to me as an interested and trained observer, that a lot of young punks get hold of a paperback about the art of disabling the opposition. He—the young punk—reads it, and then he thinks, "Oh gee, there's a real packet of money to be made out of this!" So then he has a wonderful idea, he will re-write the book as a correspondence course, and then he will get his girl friend topless and almost bottomless as well and he will have some photographs taken showing how a small girl can throw a big man. Then the advertisement is put in suitable, gullible publications, and the money comes pouring in, and the suckers really queue up to put their money into something which really isn't suitable for them.

People ask me what I think of it, and I have a standard question. It is: "All right, you are being mugged after you have taken five lessons of a self-defence course, but what are you going to do if you attacker has taken ten lessons? If he gets too much opposition from you—if you make his act of robbery too troublesome, then he is really going to beat you up, whereas previously he would only take your money."

The Police, I believe almost without any exception, advise a person to keep quiet, not to put up any opposition, because if a mugger or robber is desperate and he meets opposition, then quite likely what was going to have been a simple act of robbery could turn into rape or actual mutilation. It could even turn into murder. If you do not resist a robber but instead observe very carefully what he is like, how big he is; is he tall, thin, fat, any particular mannerisms, what is his speech like? Look at him carefully, study him—without appearing to do so— so that you can give the Police a good accurate description of the attacker. You must be able to describe him accurately, the colour of his hair, for instance, colour of eyes, the shape of his mouth and ears, and any special peculiarities, for instance, does it appear that he is left-handed, does he limp, is there some distinctive item of dress which would enable you to identify him after? Remember, if he is arrested on your description you may have to go the Police Station and identify him in a Police line-up, and you won't half look stupid if you identify a plain-clothes Policeman who has been stuck in there just to add to the number! So my strong advice is keep calm, don't panic, and observe the attacker or robber very carefully making mental notes of anything worthwhile.

The best advice I can give you is—don't go in for these silly cults, they won't do you any good.

Another thing that people write to me about is these weapons which are advertised in so many magazines nowadays. It is usually for a thing that looks like a fountain pen, it is about the size of a fountain pen, and it is advertised as protection against attackers. It is a gas gun. You just wait until you are attacked and then you grab this apparent fountain pen and press the end. From the other end there emerges a cloud of noxious gas which will disable a person for perhaps twenty to thirty minutes.

In theory this is a wonderful idea for protecting YOU, but think; can you be sure that wind conditions are right for YOU? If the wind is blowing against you the gas cloud will not go out to your attacker but will gas you, and the attacker will have the biggest laugh of his life as he sees you writhing on the ground under the influence of your own defence weapon. All he's got to do then is to bend down, take your watch, any jewellery you have, and you are quite helpless, there is nothing you can do about it. So—a strong, strong piece of advice is—when you see these advertisements for gas guns just smile with superior knowledge, and do not buy. You may be laying a trap for yourself if you do buy.

Remember this; the Police are trained to find robbers, they are trained to deal with attaekers, and if you go and try to defend yourself then you will find that if you get thoroughly beat up or your throat slit, or something else, you won't get much sympathy from the Police or from anyone else. Leave it to the Police, that's the safest way.

I am very, very unhappy about some of the advertisements which appear in various publications nowadays. For instance, people often send me advertisements which indicate that some crummy little firm has been advertising that they are making items specially designed by Lobsang Rampa, or—items which are made in Lobsang Rampa's workshop. Let me, then, get this clear now once and for all; I do not make any items at all, I have no workshop. Instead I spend most of my time in bed or in a wheelchair, and I have no facilities and no inclination for making anything of this nature.

I have no business enterprises of any kind whatsoever, and I am not connected with any firm at all, not connected directly nor indirectly. There are two people only who can in any way use my name; they are Mr. Sowter of A Touch Stone Ltd., 33 Ashby Road, Loughborough, Leicestershire, England, and Mr. Ed Orlowski of Covehead, York P.O., P.E.I., Canada. For these two people I have designed certain things and given them permission to manufacture AS BEING DESIGNED BY ME AND MADE BY THEM. Now, apart from those two people no one else at all has any right to claim that they are associated with me or are making items of my design. If they do claim that they have items of mine and they are not called Sowter or Orlowski, then you can be sure they are definite out and out frauds.

I mention this because there have been so many of these sprouting evil growths advertising in psychic magazines. They advertise as if they are associated with me, as if they are bosom friends of mine, whereas, actually, they are usually quite the reverse. So will you keep that in mind? You have been warned!

CHAPTER SIX

Conditions had been very trying of late. There had been a terrible influx of letters, sometimes well over a hundred letters each day, and people got so irritated if they had to wait a day or two for a reply.

The pains had been increasing and the general type of weather had been making me feel worse and worse. Night after night I tossed restlessly in my hospital bed at home, and at last one night I couldn't stand it any longer.

Mrs. Rampa nearly burned out the telephone lines trying to find a doctor who would do a house call. One awful woman doctor was most discourteous and most inhumane: "Take him off to hospital," she said, "it's the only thing to do with people like that." Well, my wife phoned around and phoned around place after place, but no doctor was willing to do a house call.

I passed the night in truly considerable agony wondering whatever had happened to the medical profession. Surely the medical profession was dedicated to the relief of suffering, surely one of the elementary precepts was "Do no harm". It was, indeed, doing me harm leaving me in my state of suffering, but for that night there was to be no relief, no ease. The dismal hours wore on and all through the night the traffic roared by my window. One of the remarkable things about Calgary is that traffic continues unabated throughout the twenty-four hours, it seems that the traffic never ceases, but that is to be expected of a city which has the greatest number of cars to the population in North America.

At last the first dim glimmerings of light began to filter in my window, and then once again there was the effort to try to find a doctor who would do a house call. Some of you may wonder why I wasn't rushed off to hospital. The answer to that is simple; hospitals nowadays do not like to take a patient unless there is a definite order, or committal from a General Practitioner. There have been so many cases reported lately of patients being turned away from hospitals, in fact, just about the time of my increasing illness a case had been reported of a person who had been taken to hospital and who had been refused. The poor wretched sufferer had been taken to a number of hospitals and refused from each one, and then he died at home. At the Inquest it all came out, but because I was ill at the time I rather lost track of what happened although I believe the whole thing was hushed-up by the hospital authorities.

At about midday we were successful in getting a doctor call upon me. He came, he looked, and he phoned the ambulance. In about twenty minutes the ambulance men came, and very smart, very efficient young men they were. They were the most considerate ambulance men I have had, and I have been in hospitals in England, Germany, France, Russia and a few other places. But these young men really knew their job. They got me on their mobile stretcher and they got me out of the door, and then one of them said proudly, "You're only the second patient to ride in this ambulance, its only been delivered to us today." Yes, and a nice ambulance it was, too. My stretcher was slid inside, one of the attendants got in with me, and off we drove to the Foothills Hospital.

Soon we were rolling along the new road leading to the hospital. Soon after there was a sudden darkening as we entered the Ambulance bay. Without any red tape, without any lost time, my stretcher was slid out and on to the wheeled trolley again, and the two ambulance men pushed me through corridors and into an elevator.

Smoothly the elevator moved upwards and came to a stop without a jerk. I was manoeuvred most carefully down another corridor and into a ward, and I must again say that these two young men knew their job, they were efficient, they were gentle, so different from some others from whom I have suffered.

The Foothills Hospital is perhaps the best hospital in Calgary, the most efficient, the most modern. It is a "warm" place where people "care," and I must say that the time I spent there was as pleasant as the nurses and orderlies could make it. No one is going to be so foolish as to say that the treatment is pleasant, it is as I said to the Income Tax people when they tried to query why I should have a wheelchair—well, surely one doesn't have a wheelchair for pleasure, it is a matter of necessity for the disabled—and in the same way the treatment in the hospital was not enjoyable but it was made as painless as possible by the care and devotion of the medical staff.

At other hospitals there has been absolutely no human thought, but for the Foothills Hospital—I was so impressed that when I left I wrote to the Medical Director and Administrator specifically praising certain nurses and a certain orderly, an orderly who really did go beyond the limit of his strict duty to make things easier for sufferers.

Naturally enough, I hope I never go in the Foothills

Hospital again, but undoubtedly I shall have to go to a hospital and my choice without any reservations would be that one again—the Foothills Hospital of Calgary, about the best hospital that one can meet—if one does meet a hospital!

But home again, not cured, naturally. I was feeling quite ill and the work on this book is hard going, hard going because when one has had as much suffering as I have had then the body rebels at extra work. Never mind, I have said that this book will be written, and it will be written.

Today I have been out again for the second time since I came home from the hospital. Biggs is still here, and will be here for about a week more. We went up into the foothills and once again I discovered the disadvantages of being a "sensitive" because we passed an old Indian encampment, the scene of a massacre, and the worse I am in health the more psychic I become and at one stage I had to close my eyes because I could "see" the Indians and the battle raging. It was so vivid that it was, to me, as plain as was the car in which I sat, and it is a frightening thing to go driving through a massacre.

Even Biggs, the driver, not claiming to be a "sensitive", could still feel something as if his hair was standing on end.

It was very pleasant, though, up in the higher ground looking out across the city. But, like so many other cities nowadays, the atmosphere is polluted. We have oil wells all around Calgary and they spew fumes into the air day and night. In my ignorance I always marvel that the fumes lie around the city. We are 3,500 feet above sea level, the highest city in Canada, and I rather wondered why the fumes didn't go rolling down to the Prairies. Never mind, one day perhaps I shall know the reason, but it is disheartening to look out and to see this ring of brown fog all around the city.

Back from my tour into the foothills—work again because the work must go on no matter what.

Before we go on answering the type of questions in which you are mostly interested, let me answer a question which is very frequently put to me:—"I just don't understand this address of yours, BM/TLR, London, England, doesn't seem much of an address to me." People do not believe that that is a proper address and so they engage in all manner of strange devices to make sure that the Post Office authorities in England know that the letter is meant for me. So I am going to take a little space to give a free advertisement to a very fine firm.

Many, many years ago a man in England decided that it would be a wonderful convenience for travellers and others who did not want their address commonly known to have an arrangement with the British Post Office whereby he could have a general address which was British Monomarks, London W.C. 1, and any correspondence bearing the BM would be sent to a firm which he organized.

Then for a very modest sum he provided people with what are called Monomark addresses. The cheapest type are those which are allotted to one which could be, by way of example, BM/1234. But if you want to use your own initials you could do as I have done, my Monomark is BM/TLR. Now, the BM stands for British Monomarks, and when the Post Office sorters see the BM they know it is for British Monomarks and, of course, the letter is then delivered to British Monomarks. British Monomarks know that the BM is their bit, and so they go by the second bit—TLR in this case. So they put TLR mail in a box and about two or three times a week the mail is sent on to me either by having sticky labels stuck over the BM bit or by being packed in a big envelope, it depends on what one wants.

There is another type of BM Monomark too, but that is a BCM and that is for firms, it means a commercial Monomark. Mine is a private type but if I was a big firm I would have a British Commercial Monomark. In twenty years I have not had a single complaint against British Monomarks, and it is truly a matter of complete amazement to me how carefully they deal with the mail and how infallible they are. Just think, I get a vast amount of mail from all over the world—even from Moscow!—and Monomarks don't pinch the foreign stamps off the envelopes and they don't make any mistakes, either. So if you want to find out more about them all you have to do is to write to BCM/MONO, London W.C.1, England, and they will give you all the information you need. But I want to take this opportunity of most sincerely congratulating the Monomark firm for the absolutely wonderful service they give. Take my own case; I move about, I have been to other countries and I have been all around Canada, and yet all I have to do is to write to Monomarks and tell them that as from such-and-such a date please forward all mail to (my new address), and without any mistakes whatever the mail arrives.

Let me tell you this, it's worth telling, or worth reading; a little time ago there was a most unfortunate occurrence. A lady of my acquaintance—a friend of mine—had a little nerve trouble and, I suppose, she was worried about the troubles I was having with the press. So she wrote to British Monomarks and told them to send all my mail to her address. She made it appear that it was a definite request from me.

British Monomarks are truly an experienced firm. They did not take her at her word, they were not deluded . . . they wrote to me to see what my instructions were. Well, I nearly blew a fuse, but then I calmed down and realized that you don't just throw over a friend for a little mistake caused perhaps by nerve strain, so I told Monomarks to send my mail on to me as before. Really I cannot praise them too highly. You may think I am "going overboard" about them, but that is not so at all. One's mail is important, and it is vital to all of us that we can absolutely depend on those who forward our mail. You CAN depend on Monomarks! So—thank you, ladies and gentlemen of the Monomark Staff.

Mrs. Rouse—alias Buttercup—tells me I look like Doc of the Seven Dwarfs when I am getting ready for work. Well, I am not sure she doesn't really mean Dopey, but anyway I suppose I do look a queer old fellow stuck in a wheelchair surrounded by masses of letters containing even more masses of questions. Never mind, I have been asked to write this book, and I am writing the thing in spite of feeling like something the cat brought in—and left behind in a hurry. So let's get on with our questions and answers, shall we?

Oh glory be, oh glory be—I've let myself in for something now! Here is the first question which I have just picked up, so you'd better sit back and polish up your glasses if you wear the things, and get a load of this: "Considering we are three dimensional beings evolving (hopefully) into the fourth dimension, it follows logically that we came from a second dimension and before that a first. The first question is, is this digression true, and if so what were we before the first dimension, and what spiritual attainment did we need to advance. Now, to further complicate things, if the first and second do not exist in our evolution as we theorized before then where do we originate from before the third dimension!?"

Now, I hope your head is not going around as much as mine is because actually this is true enough, you know, we do evolve from a one dimensional being. Consider, for example, an amoeba. You could logically, I suppose, consider the lowly amoeba as being a one dimensional creature, and all life evolves from a single-celled entity, and the single cell grows other cells and then eventually fission occurs to make two or more entities. That is the earliest stage of evolution. But anyway, actually, this is not a question that we can answer satisfactorily because the one dimensional creature would have no more understanding of our third dimensional world than a person can have of the sixth dimensional world while here. So we have to take certain things on trust. There are some people who really blind themselves with science, as the saying is. They try to formulate questions beyond their own understanding. So—we do evolve from a one dimensional entity right up to uncountable, unmentionable dimensions until at last we become one with the Overself, and then when we are one with the Overself the Overself is complete, and then it too has to go on to further evolution. You cannot have things stationary in any form of nature, nothing is stationary. You can't stand still on a tightrope, for instance. If you try to you've got to keep on wobbling or swaying in order to maintain your apparently stationary posture, and if you are wobbling you are not stationary, are you? So all life is movement, all life is vibration, and the more we evolve the more vibrations we set into motion.

Would it help at all if I say to the musicians we can have one simple note, middle C, if you like (that's the only one I know!), and then you can take that as being a

95

one dimensional being. But then when you progress so that you can use two hands on your piano and you can play a multiple chord, you can say that you are now up to three, or four, or five dimensions in terms of vibration, because, whether we like it or not, music no matter how beautiful is still just a collection of vibrations which "get on" with each other.

I am sorry I can't answer that more specifically, but you would not teach newborn babies the calculus, would you?

Now here is a question which is sure to get me in trouble. Some people write and tell me that I am opposed to Jews. Believe me, that is definitely not the case! I get on extremely well with Jewish people, I suppose as a Buddhist I have some sympathy with them; most of them certainly have sympathy with me.

"You have said that Jewish people are a group who were kept back to try it again in this Round of existence. Does this mean that Jewish people are always Jews throughout their lives on Earth?"

No, it doesn't mean that at all. Let's forget about Jews and Christians and Buddhists, let's have a look at a school. All right, we are in our school; we've got a bunch of Grade Two hoodlums and they have reached the end of term, now they are being put through their paces by way of examinations to see if their stupid brains have absorbed any knowledge during the past term. Some of them can pass the examinations, probably through good fortune more than anything else. But, anyway, the ones who pass go up to Grade Three. The poor wretches who do not pass get kept in Grade Two. Now, when they are in Grade Two for the second time they feel inferior and superior at the same time. They feel inferior in that they were not brainy enough to pass the examinations and get promoted, but they feel superior to the new crowd who have come into Grade Two, and so sometimes they act in a most unbearable manner. You feel it would be a pleasure to take a cane and tan their backsides until they turned into leather.

Jews are people who, on another Round of existence or another Cycle of existence—call it what you will—did not pass the end of term examinations, so they have been kept back in this particular class for another go, and some of them feel arrogant, some of them feel inferior, but the rest of the people resent the Jews because they have so much more innate knowledge.

I get on with Jews very well, I understand them, they understand me, and no Jew has ever tried to convert me to anything. Gentiles have. Sometimes stupid old biddies with a touch of religious mania make life a misery by sending me tracts, pamphlets, Bibles, "good words" in verse—and they get worse and worse—and all the rest. Sometimes they will send me ornamental crucifixes or pictures which I am supposed to hang up all around me. Well, all the junk of that sort goes in the garbage, I don't need anyone to tell me what my religion is going to be. I have one even though I am a Buddhist—I have my own private beliefs, Buddhism is just a way of life.

Anyway, Jews are nearly always far better behaved than Christians, aren't they? Look at Jewish children, how well they are disciplined. Look at Jewish adults. If they are treated properly they are fine people, and I am proud to number certain wonderful Jewish people as my friends.

There weren't any Jews before Abraham, anyway, or they weren't called Jews before that. Before that they had a completely different classification. One might say the G.I. Joe suddenly becomes Joe Doakes, it's just a case of being a rose by another name.

So a short answer would be that a person is not necessarily a Jew after this particular cycle because after he has "learned his lessons" he will be promoted to the next class where—hopefully—there won't even be Christians. Look at it like this—in school a second grader is one who couldn't pass his examinations but if at the next examinations he does pass then he might be promoted to a third grade.

One lady is having trouble, it seems. She wants to know, "Is there herbal birth control that you know of? Is there any form you would recommend that is practised now?"

I have never set up as a birth control specialist and, of course, people in Far Eastern countries use only herbs to control conception and these herbs are infallible. But what is the point, madam, of telling you about them if you can't go out and get them—and you can't. So I think the kindest advice I can give you is that if you feel "that way" you'd better go along to your local birth control clinic and get their advice.

Oh, tut tut, dear me. Some people get really nasty at times, don't they? I've got a "gentleman" here who tells me in the most vicious way possible that I am out to make a "fast buck" writing books and if I were in any way genuine I would see that a special Index was prepared so that he wouldn't have the trouble (HE, mind you!) of looking through all my books to find out something hidden in a mass of stupid words.

Well, of course, I would like to have an Index but no one else seems to want it. I would like, in fact, to have a separate book such as, for example, a sixteenth book, and the sixteenth book would be nothing but an Index. All

98

right, then, would you Readers be prepared to pay for a book which was nothing but an Index? If so write and tell my publisher. You will find the address in this book. He won't provide it free, that's certain, because he too has to make a living. Anyway, if people read my books properly they should have an adequate knowledge of what is in them. Did I tell you I had had a letter from a woman in California, she told me that she had read "You —Forever" in half an hour, and if I was anything of a writer I would put all the meat of the book in half a chapter!! I am still marvelling that a person can read a book such as "You—Forever" in half an hour—still marvelling and still disbelieving.

A gentleman in France seems to be very worried about his future. He tells me that, "Perhaps I have evil put my question to you but they seem to have provoked you a little paradoxical answers opposite which you in your books express. Far be it from me to address a reproach to you, but on the contrary a fervent desire for weel to understand you. You say in your letter that the Mediterranean will be quite safe, on the other hand I believe to remember that in the one of your books you speak of submersion for the perifery of the sea."

Well, I still say I am right. The Mediterranean will eventually have the seabed rise so that what is now water will become land. I told this enquirer in a letter that he would be quite safe, and I still say that he will be quite safe from such a disaster. You see, people think of their own lifetime and they think that that is all eternity, but it isn't. If a catastrophe is going to happen in perhaps a hundred years then a person who might have, perhaps, twenty years of life left is quite safe from that disaster. People write to me and ask me if they should flee to the Rockies or should they go somewhere else, and they get quite offensive when I tell them that in my opinion they will be quite safe where they are. Think of an old fellow of seventy writing to me in a horrible state of fright because he thinks the land is going to sink and he is going to get the top of his head wet. I say that where the man lives there will be submergence IN THE YEARS TO COME, but I do not think that there will be a submergence in his lifetime. If you are thinking of your grandsons, okay—move out fast, move into the Rockies, the Canadian Rockies of course. You will have to do a lot of snow clearing first because as I am writing this book I can look out and see the Rockies and there really is a pile of snow at the top. But, seriously, the average person who writes in doesn't have to worry, these disasters won't be in your lifetime unless you are writing on behalf of a small child!

Hello Shelagh McMorran, so you have decided to send me some questions, have you? You ask me, "What must one do to be able to communicate with Nature Spirits or fairies?"

That's easy enough. You have to live what is called a "pure life" in order that your vibrations are increased. You have to live as a hermit (hermitess?) because if you mix with a lot of people your personal vibrations will be slowed down otherwise you won't be able to get on with other people.

Then you will have to practise telepathy because it's no good speaking to Nature Spirits in vocal words. The vocal system of speech is too crude, too gross, for Nature Spirits. All you can use is telepathy. But if you can communicate with your cat then you can communicate with Nature Spirits.

You also say, "People cast about looking for salvation

and enlightenment. Could it be that the answers we seek lie not in any outside source but only within us?"

Oh yes, definitely. We are what we make ourselves. If we believe in a thing then that thing can be, and I would say that by far the easiest method of finding "salvation" is to obey the Golden Rule—Do only unto others as you would have them do unto you.

So many people think they are going to get salvation in some holy book or by following some Teaching which is thousands of years out of date. If you are going to follow some of these early Christian beliefs then you will have to agree that women are inferior articles, chattels. But our Women's Libbers wouldn't like that, and, of course, they are right. My own belief is (should I whisper it?) women are in every way the equal of men but they are different creatures, almost a different species. Men are suitable for some things, women are suitable for others. So why don't women do their particular task and look after the nation, look after the discipline and training of the forthcoming race? They would find they would get salvation that way!

"Humbleness, sincerity, harmlessness, forgiveness, uprightness, devotion to the spiritual master, purity, steadiness, self-harmony . . . if a person is trying to live these precepts could he (or pardon me, also she) have faith that he is progressing rightly even though no visions are seen and no occult powers are made manifest?"

Definitely, because if you are obeying the Golden Rule then you will be on the way to getting all these abilities, and there is nothing "holy" in being psychic, there is nothing particularly spiritual in being clairvoyant, it is just an ability. For example, you wouldn't say that a person is necessarily spiritual because she can sing or paint or write books, they are abilities. Spirituality has nothing to do with it, so it doesn't matter how pure or holy or upright a person may be, if he or she does not have the necessary physical make-up to be psychic then he or she won't be psychic. You can be psychic even if you are bad, but it's better to be psychic and good.

Now, Shelagh McMorran has a question here which applies to a lot of people, a lot of people have written similar type of things, so here's the complete question:— "It has been said by you and other wise men that when the student is ready the Teacher will appear. It has also been said that for one to progress on the Path and awaken the latent divinity within oneself one must have a Teacher. How best may one prepare for the meeting with a spiritual Teacher, can this meeting take place in any walk of life or must certain things be done or given up before it can take place? Would it be true that one might prepare now for a meeting to take place in some future life?"

Yes, it is perfectly true that when the student is ready the Teacher will appear, and it is not for the student to say when he or she is ready. What happens is this; as the aspiring student develops he or she (oh, bother, let's just say "he" as a generic term) increases in basic vibration. That vibration is like a bell sounding in the etheric, so a Teacher who is always ready for a student, and who may appear in the physical or who may not, goes to the aid of a student. And I want to make it clear that it doesn't necessarily mean that the Teacher is going to sit opposite the student and rap him over the knuckles every so often to secure his attention; the Teacher may be in the astral and may teach the student when the student also is in the astral.

So many people write and insist that they are ready— they are quite positive that they are ready—so why do

102

not I or someone else rush over land and sea to their assistance?

I dispute that people should have physical Teachers. I am definitely opposed to all these correspondence courses alleging to teach one metaphysics, spirituality, etc., etc. If you need a Teacher you will get one in the astral, and I'm going to tell you this; when you die, that is, when your physical body is finished with this Earth and your astral entity goes on to the astral world it has to stand alone and answer for successes and failures, and it is useless to think that because you once took a correspondence course in boot licking that the chief bootlicker is going to come and speak on your behalf explaining why you can only lick black boots and not brown boots. No, when you pass over you have to stand alone and answer to yourself alone, so the best thing to do is to get used to it now, rely on yourself, rely on your own resources. You don't want to be just a slave or shadow of some correspondence course or some stupid cult leader, do you? You are an entity so act as one.

You ask, Shelagh McMorran, if certain things have to be given up before one can advance, and the answer is of course—yes. You have to give up things like intoxicants because they can affect your psyche. You have to give up drugs . . . not YOU, of course, because you don't have these things, perhaps I should have said "one" must give up these things. One must give up the things which harm the astral body because if you are harming the astral body then all your vibrations are wrong, aren't they, and if your vibrations are wrong you will not get an astral or physical Teacher, so you are back where you started from.

"Throughout the ages Initiation has played a vital role in the progress of a soul. In the present age how, and

103

under what circumstances, may this Initiation take place?"

Well, I am not much in favour of initiations because usually it is just a mumbo-jumbo ceremony which doesn't mean a thing except to scare some poor wretch half out of his life. All you need, really, is a simple straightforward affirmation, a statement of intent, a promise that one is going to do certain things or study certain things, and I maintain that it is just plain stupid to dunk a person in dirty water or give him a swig of wine, or put bits of coloured cloth on him. That merely is a theatrical act of mumbo-jumbo. A simple affirmation is all that is necessary as an initiation ceremony. It is merely an understanding that a person is ready to take certain steps which will increase his psychic ability.

"Jesus and other World Leaders had followers and friends other than their immediate disciples. You have said in 'Chapters of Life' that a new World Leader is to be born in 1985. Would it be possible for a person to do anything now to be worthy of becoming a helper, supporter, follower or friend to the new World Leader in that future time, or will those close followers all be on a different cycle from the rest of us?"

The only way that one can prepare is by living a decent life, a spiritual life, a "correct" life, and so setting an example to those around you. Nowadays we live in a truly horrid age where everybody is trying to beat down everyone else, and things are going to get much worse unless enough of us make sure that we are examples of the benefits that can be derived by leading a decent life. Most people will only do a thing if there is some material gain for them. That sounds shockingly cynical, I know, but I believe it to be a fact, and so at the outset at least

104

one has to show others that there are material benefits from calmness, peacefulness, and honesty, and until the "opposition" can be convinced of those benefits then they will not follow the strait and narrow Path.

CHAPTER SEVEN

Buttercup has just been reminding me that I am not doing much toward answering psychic questions so far in this book. I don't know what I am supposed to have been doing, then, because I thought that that was what the book was all about. Anyway, how about this for a question? "How would a person know if the Kundalini had begun to rise other than by having his aura observed?"

The person would know, and if the Kundalini had risen through the result of wrong practices the psychiatrist would know also! If a person meddles with the Kundalini—and he can—then he can induce very severe mental disturbance. A person should never try to raise the Kundalini but should always wait for it to occur naturally. It is a very dangerous thing indeed to interfere with the Kundalini.

Of course one can observe the aura and see what is happening to the aura and to the Kundalini, but then we come back to the old problem of how to part people from their panties. It is a most extraordinary thing because as I write this in an extremely hot temperature of 90 degrees there are people out in their swimming pools or paddling pools or whatever they call the things, and some of them are barely clad. It seems that they will take off most of their clothes for the sake of display, but when it comes to a serious thing like studying the aura—no, they would like to have clothes painted on. Anyway, by what I have seen of people around in nearby bathing pools it's a darn good thing some of these women do keep their clothes on, they would look better in a completely shapeless garment than they do in their bikini things, or whatever they call them. It reminds me of fat women with tight pants—ohhh!—but I'd better not get on a subject like that!!

Another question, "Is it possible in the present age to have the third eye opened in the manner in which you did, or must this be the result of gradual awakening of the chakras?"

Well, would you have your appendix removed by an amateur? Or would you do it yourself? If you've got any sense, and you must have or you wouldn't be reading this book, you would try to get the best specialist you could to do the job for you. In the same way, you would need to get a real specialist to open your third eye, and they are about as rare as raspberries on gooseberry bushes in the West. Actually, it is not at all a difficult matter if one can look at the aura at the same time because by looking at the aura one can tell precisely what is happening, and so it is possible to control everything.

Actually, though, I would never, never advise a Western person to have the third eye opened by operation. In the same way I advise Western people not to have acupuncture. It works just fine for Easterners because they have been brought up to it and because in many ways they are quite a lot different from Westerners. So—don't have your third eye opened by operation or you may end up spiritually blind.

Someone here is interested in pendulums ... oh, it's our friend Shelagh McMorran. She writes, "Would it be possible or likely for an elemental or somesuch to control the responses of a pendulum?"

Yes, its quite possible for mischievous entities to do almost anything, they could easily control the pendulum, for instance. In case you wonder how this can be, let me say that a man is driving a school bus; now, he's got a rowdy lot of school kids with him and after a time they might whisper together and gang up on the driver. Then one schoolboy, more foolish or more adventurous than others, would take hold of the steering wheel and try to control it in spite of the driver's efforts. It might even be that some of the other boys would even pull the driver's hands from the wheel. Kids nowadays will do just about everything so why shouldn't they do that? But that is a similar state to when a mischievous entity takes over control of the pendulum. The user of the pendulum for some reason has lost control, or never had it, and that is why I always stress that you should make the pendulum yours and no one else's, because if YOU control the pendulum no other entity can possibly do so, so it all depends on how much control you have.

Now, here is a question . . .

"In 'Chapters of Life' you made predictions about events which will occur during this end period of the present world cycle. During this period do you think the Gardeners of the Earth will return to weed and prune this tangled and twisted garden, or is it more likely they will return after the cataclysms have taken care of most of we weeds (or is it us weeds?)?"

It is my belief that the Gardeners of the Earth are getting heartily sick of conditions on this world because, you know, humans, basically, are getting more and more selfish and instead of people trying to do each other a good turn they nowadays seem bent for destruction.

107

I believe that round about (I said "round about") the year 2000 we may see quite startling incidents during which, possibly, the Gardeners of the Earth or their special messengers will come to take a look at our world.

In past cataclysms the surface people of the Earth were driven so they could enter the interior of the Earth through the large holes at the Poles. Naturally, people inside the Earth will be quite safe from atom bombs which devastate the exterior because I believe that the thickness of the Earth between this and the inner layer is 800 to 1,000 miles, much of it iron ore and various hard rocks.

If you want to see the fun, then, hang around until round about the year 2000 then you will get a free firework display.

Now for a complete change of theme. This is a question from a South American country, and the question is a very sensible one. It is, "When praying what should I really call my Overself? I do not like a human name, would it be all right to say 'God', 'Lord', or 'Guide', or just 'Overself'? You have mentioned that the Overself has several puppets to manage, does that mean he manages other people as well and not only me? Then it is not only my Overself but also other peoples. Are these people in any way related to me or not?"

Well, that's a stunner! I started out thinking that was one question, instead it's a whole bunch of questions, isn't it? Never mind, let's get on with it; it really does not matter what you call your Overself any more than it matters what you call your sub-conscious because so long as you get over the idea that you are addressing the Overself or that you are addressing the sub-conscious, then you could even have a number, number one for Overself, number two for sub-conscious. Of course, that is not necessarily too facetious because it just doesn't matter what you call the Overself provided that you are consistent. You must always use the same name.

Now, I have mentioned many times about the Overself and the puppets. Let's put it this way; you have your body, let's call your body the Overself. And then you have a right hand, a left hand, a right foot and a left foot, let's call them your puppets. So your hands and feet are definitely part of you, aren't they, they are definitely related to each other, so in precisely the same way the other people who are the puppets of that one Overself are related, are connected, are dependent upon each other. And the Overself has to manage each of those puppets in the same way that you have to manage your hands and your feet. For example, if your feet can't get on together you can't walk because supposing the puppets which you call your feet disliked each other and both tried to take a right step at the same time, well you would fall over backwards. I'm not sure it couldn't be done, and I'm certainly not going to try, but you have to keep your hands and your feet on a good working relationship with each other.

Now this question, "When leaving this life *must* we all pass the place where those elementals, thought forms, or whatever they are try to scare us? Is that something inevitable for all of us, or do the helpers have a chance to save us from that? If we should die suddenly, for example, by some traffic accident or aeroplane crash, etc., do the helpers have time to get to us at once or must we then drift alone prey to those awful elementals?"

Say! I seem to have fallen on a bunch of multiple questions. Now what have I done to deserve this? Well, anyway, suppose you are going to travel by train or car or bus or aeroplane, then you have to cross a certain area of "public domain" before you get into your vehicle. For instance, suppose you have a car outside your house and you want to get in that car. You have to get out of your house and you have to cross the sidewalk to get in to your vehicle. In the same way, when you leave your body you have to cross an area of "public domain for spirits" to get into the astral, but in ninety-nine percent of the cases you do not see any elementals. If you are not afraid then you have nothing to worry about because if you are not afraid then the elementals can't bother you, they can't approach you. So what is there to worry about, anyway? You might be leaving your house and proceeding to your car and you might see a lot of gaping children at the sidewalk, but you don't have to bother about them, do you? So why bother about elementals?

And yes, most certainly helpers have a chance to save you from anything. It doesn't matter if you have a sudden crash, the helpers are still there, because you must remember that time on Earth is a purely artificial thing and it has no meaning elsewhere. For instance, if you wanted to go from, say, South America to Australia while on the Earth you would have quite a commotion getting tickets, packing up your things, and actually travelling from South America to Australia. You would have all sorts of customs and immigration formalities. But in this other state in the astral, you think of a place and you are there, it's as quick as that. So that a person in the astral can be an uncountable distance from you in miles but he could say, "Oh my goodness, there's Jim Bugsbottom about to have an accident, I'm going." And then the astral helper would be there at the scene of the accident even before the thing happened.

Now for another question about astrals. "You have mentioned at least two different astral stages in the

110

former books, one a little higher than the other, as far as I have understood. Do we all, average, not so evolved people have to go there after dying to Earth? Is it on that plane there can exist a sort of family life you also mentioned in some of the books? Is it possible to graduate directly from one plane to a higher one, or must we all inevitably reincarnate between each higher astral plane?"

If you could look in on me now you would see that I was looking gloomier and gloomier. For one thing the temperature is getting hotter and hotter—it really IS a hot day here—and for another thing here is another of these darn multiple questions. I feel that I am writing three or four books at once!

We on Earth are in a certain stage of evolution. Here we are in a physical stage in a third dimensional world. When we "die", that is, when our body ceases to function for some reason, we go to "the astral plane," that is a sort of reception area, and in that particular astral plane we make an assessment of what we have done and what we have left undone upon the third dimensional world, we take advice from special counsellors, and perhaps we may decide that it will be better if we return to Earth, that is, reincarnate and have another life on Earth.

It may be, though, that we haven't done so badly after all, and in that case we shall be able to advance—to go to a higher plane of existence, perhaps a fourth dimensional, perhaps a fifth dimensional world. But I must again express that time is different when one is off the Earth, and one can stay a long time in the astral and then reincarnate almost instantly according to Earth days on this world. It is very confusing if you are too accustomed to believing that time is a hard and fast 60 seconds to the minute, 60 minutes to the hour, 24 hours to the day, etc. Time in the astral is flexible, but in the astral we can have

111

our friendly associations, in fact we have to have them in order to round out our basic experiences. We can also have suitable love affairs—I'm sure that will cheer up a lot of you!

It really seems that some poor fellow is all gummed up about this astral business. Look at this for a question; "If one of my children, or any loved one, should leave this Earth before me or after me, and that person is then sent back to Earth in a new incarnation before I arrive there, or I am sent back before they arrive, how is it possible for us then to meet in the astral? And if they or I should have graduated to a higher astral plane how can we then meet? Is it possible to visit one another even being on separate astral planes?"

Throughout my books I have tried to put over the idea of astral travel, I have tried to get over to people the thought that they can if they want leave this body and go into the astral plane and meet people in the astral plane. It seems I have not succeeded too well, doesn't it? So if the person who asks these questions will read my books— well, the answer is there plain enough; if you want to meet a person in the astral then you can, by telepathy, arrange such a meeting, and you can get out of your body for that purpose.

If a person is in a higher plane and he or she wants to meet you in the astral, he or she can travel downwards to your own astral plane. There is no problem at all provided that both persons want such a meeting.

I have just been looking at another question and wonder if I should quietly drop everything and retire to a monastery. Perhaps in view of some of these questions it would be more appropriate to retire to a nunnery. Anyway, you judge for yourself. Here is the question, and how would YOU answer it?

"At what stage exactly, or more or less exactly, does the spirit enter a baby to be born? There are thousands of women on this Earth with that question on their mind. Some have been blindly, romantically in love and have been led too far by the boy or man that confessed eternal true love and marriage but couldn't dominate his passion, and so the tragedy has occurred. He still loves her but cannot yet afford to marry her and she must get rid of it, etc. Nowadays it is probably carelessness and just indulging in sex for pleasure and not caring for anything, I don't know. But can you answer that question, do you know? Sex is not sin nor bad if connected with love, as you yourself have said in the books. Sex without love is meaningless and just animal pleasure but is still practised mostly so. Is it not murder to abort before the spirit enters the embryo of a child? When is the moment when an abortion becomes murder?"

Well, well, and well again. After being "exposed" to some of these questions I feel like one of those Aunt Fanny's who write in certain newspapers purporting to answer all assorted manner of questions. Poor souls, I know exactly how they feel. But I feel that I am being "put upon" to answer questions which are not connected with metaphysics.

I will give my own opinion, though, and it is this; if people want to know about birth control, abortion, etc., then why not go to a family planning clinic and get all the information free, and perhaps a free sample of something which will "gum up the works" for the desired time. You would find it much better to go to a family counsellor or some clinic, or to a doctor, so that you can discuss your own case and all its ramifications and all and every bit of detail about it. Then you will get information which is applicable to you and all your circumstances.

But I can't see, really, that people need to have abortions nowadays when they have so many alleged safeguards available. If they are in any doubt—well, don't!

Further, the entity who is going to take over the body does not take over at any specific time, it depends on the degree of evolution, it depends on the need, on the type, and all that sort of thing. So you could say one abortion could take place at a month and another at six months. Every case depends upon its own individual circumstances, and our Estimable Publisher will throw a fit and he might even blush if I go into any more details, so I suggest that if you do want details go to a doctor or a family planning clinic—they'll tell you all you need to know.

The temperature is getting hotter as the day wears on. I suppose it is almost a case that eggs in a shop window are becoming hard-boiled. Certainly I need to be hard-boiled to face up to some of these questions, and I am wondering whether the temperature of over 90 or the questions are the hottest. Get ready for the next one:—

"Divorce—if two people who have been in love and married and truly have believed that they would never part in this life nor in the next, little by little get hurt by each other, bewildered and desperate, and all of a sudden realize that they cannot understand each other any more but seem to develop into two strangers who are unable to communicate, what shall they do? Shall they go on living together, but almost starting to hate each other and the cleft being greater and greater, the atmosphere in the home being heavier and heavier, or shall they separate and at least not live together hating each other? How can this happen when both could swear from the bottom of their hearts that they would never stop loving each other? Each of them feels that the other one has

114

changed horribly by some mysterious fate. He and she doesn't think as before, doesn't react as before. He or she are only criticizing all the time where they before saw no fault, and when also physical problems enter in the picture and there seems to be no way out, what to do? Is it bad to separate? Should they go on living together just because they signed some documents and some priest told them to? Or should they be honest and split up and let time cure the wounds, and at last at least be able to forgive and understand that both erred, and not only one of the parts? What is wrong, what is right?"

Many people ask me this, so I will give my own honest opinion about it. I believe that in the Christian belief the priests meddle so much in marriage that everything in marriage is distorted. For example, in the Catholic belief, if a woman doesn't have enough children the priests get thoroughly unpleasant about it and threaten the husband and wife with all sorts of horrible things. I know that is true because I have seen it happen myself, and in Ireland I have learned the meaning of the old statement, "The priest had his hat on the doorknob so the husband stayed out"!

If two business partners cannot get on together, then they part. It is the only sensible thing to do, and marriage nowadays really IS a business! My personal opinion is that people should never separate; they should divorce and part definitely, deliberately, and irrevocably. After all, if you have an aching tooth you don't go to a dentist and have it half pulled, do you, you have the thing yanked straight out so that you can forget all about it. Well, if you've got wife trouble or husband trouble and you can't seem to make any sense of it, then don't waste any more time—get divorced, never mind what the stupid clod of a priest says, he is not going through it—he is not suffering—you are. I believe most of the religious muck which is blatted out nowadays is truly wrong. In the days before Christianity marriage was a most pleasant thing, different altogether to what it is now, and in religious communities not dominated by Christianity, again marriage is a more compatible affair.

The answer, then, is—divorce in a hurry. But try to part as friends who have had a difference, a disagreement. You don't have to go around ruining each other's character, it takes two people to make a divorce which means you are both to blame.

Tomorrow Mr. John Bigras—Biggs—and his two cats Mr. Wayfarer Bigras and Mrs. Wayfarer Bigras, will get in their big car and roar along toward Vancouver. I certainly wish that I could go with them riding through the mountains and seeing all the trees. Here in Calgary there are not many trees, it is far different from all the green of Vancouver. But there it is, I know that my travelling days are limited, and so first of all I must wish Mr. Bigras and Cats-Bigras bon voyage on their trip home to Vancouver. Biggs can look back on another vacation behind him for a year. Soon I shall be able to look back on a fifteenth book completed.

I get some quite extraordinary questions, for instance, how would one answer this; "I was reading in 'Cave of the Ancients' about the Japanese monk. This made me think of myself reading different things. How is one to know if we are injuring ourselves?"

Now, how can one answer that? Probably by relating all this to medicine. Let's see what we can do; suppose you have a television set and you look at all those advertisements about patent medicines, or supposing you look in the newspapers and you read the advertisements about this, that, and something else which will cure everything

—well, no one in their right senses would take all the muck advertised because so many things would not be compatible. If you took two things which were opposed, that is, not compatible, you would aggravate your condition by adding some other condition of your own making. So I can only say that if you are reading too much on too many subjects, or too much about the same subject, then you should give it a rest. Without trying to be a super-salesman, I tell people that they should read my books first because all I say in my books is true and I can do everything I write about. There has been a lot of so-called authors of late who have just lifted lumps out of other people's books and re-phrased it so it is thought to be a different book. But if you re-phrase a thing you do not always get the same meaning, do you? So—I think that a person should concentrate on one author to one subject, and when they have read all that author has written then, if they want to, they can go on to something else. But the way people go on is like those who mix their drinks which I am reliably assured is a most reprehensible practice!

Now, here is another question which really doesn't have an answer:—

"When you move to an apartment and sense something uneasy or negative what is it and how can you rid the place of it?"

I can only assume that the question means what can one do if one goes to an apartment which is haunted or which is saturated with the negative influences of the former tenants. If the place is haunted—what of it? The haunter can't hurt the hauntee, and if one exerts a definite telepathic command the haunter will go away. You see, most times a haunted building is haunted only by the dynamic vital force of a person who has passed on, the force lingers around like the last echoes of a brass band. The echoes of a brass band die away in seconds, and the echoes of a virile person's death dissipate in a second or so of astral time, which may be a hundred years of Earth time, but it can be dissipated if you give a definite telepathic command for the haunter to cease haunting.

We seem to have stumbled on a bunch this time. Look at this one—"I know someone who was into witchcraft, he soon began to feel that demons were after him so he dropped witchcraft quickly. Could you explain these demons, and how does one become possessed?"

If people mess about with witchcraft they deserve all they get and I have no sympathy with them because witchcraft is definitely tampering with forbidden forces. In the lower astral there are all sorts of entities who are like mischievous monkeys, they love imitating humans, they love teasing humans, and many many good people —people of the highest intentions—have been to seances which were not properly controlled by a trained Medium, and here these mischievous entities have relayed messages to the Medium and he or she, not knowing any better, thought they were genuine messages. Well, nothing succeeds like success, and so the more people thought that these mischievous ones were genuine so their power grew and in the end they were able to control the thoughts of the humans. They would telepathically whisper into the brain of a person that Aunt Matilda, or someone else, insisted that such-and-such a thing be done. But, again, if a person is not afraid nothing bad can happen. If you are haunted or think you are possessed then you just have to say very very firmly an affirmation that nothing can harm you and that the entity persecuting you will dissipate. These entities don't want to dissipate so they go away very quickly in search of

118

someone else who cannot banish them, so there is nothing to be frightened about except of being afraid.

"My father is a teacher in a junior high school and has a growing interest in your Teachings. He often tells me of destructive deliquency of the kids, they are supposed to be from good families. How can these kids get out of their ruts or be helped?"

I thought I had dealt with that at considerable and tedious length already because I really firmly believe that there won't be any improvement in conditions until the mothers stay at home and make the home. Nowadays children are left to wander in the streets where they fall prey to stronger companions—stronger companions who are most often bent on destruction, and so they contaminate the "kids from good families." The only way the matter can be overcome is to revamp our society so that once again motherhood is a virtue instead of an unfortunate accident.

"Yesterday a girl approached my wife and I and tried very hard to sell us her Buddhism. I told her I had another Path and that her sales pitch turned me off. How is one to be sure of which Path to follow?"

Oh, that's an easy one! The real Buddhists have no missionaries. The real Buddhists never try to persuade anyone at all to become a Buddhist. You have probably fallen foul of one of these awful cult-girls who lounge about nowadays and try to get other victims who will pay dues to some imaginary Buddhist Society. Let me say again that if anyone tried to get you to become a Buddhist then he or she is not a Buddhist because Buddhism is just a way of life and not a religion, and Buddhism has no missionaries.

There are too many cults nowadays, there is a psuedo-education in which young punks of both sexes think they are the chosen Messiah who should get recruits for this, that or some other society.

In connection with this I am going to do what I rarely do, I am going to advise you to read a particular book all about secret societies, giving the origin of some of the cults who are always advertising in the papers nowadays, cults who try to get your money for their own ends. The book is "Secret Societies" edited by Norman MacKenzie and published by Crescent Books of New York.

In my opinion this is a most excellent book and one that I thoroughly recommend. I wish I had written it myself!

"Wayne and I are vegans. We follow Professor Arnold Ehrets diet. It consists of fruit and vegetables, no animal products, and nuts. I often wondered what you might have to say about it. Is it a diet that leads to freedom from disease, as the Professor believes? Also I am anxious to have people such as yourself get complete nutrition from barley, tea and butter. What do you think of this diet?"

If I really told you what I thought the publisher would probably fall off his chair in a dead faint because my thoughts on such things are incendiary. I think these crackpot diets are bunk, I think they are real muck. The U.S. military forces had a long trial of people taking the ordinary everyday military diet and those crackpots who went in for vegetarianism, you know, a cabbage leaf and a handful of nuts and things like that. Well, after six months the American authorities discovered quite definitely that the vegetarians were inferior in everything, inferior in brain power, inferior in physique, inferior in endurance, and definitely no more healthy.

On this Earth we are animals, and as we are animals and behave like animals we should eat that which our animal bodies demand. So if you take muck like this stupid diet and you find that your health is deteriorating you have no one but yourself to blame. I have no sympathy whatever with all these crackpot, stupid diets which have never been proved to be anything but a cult.

"I have just bought 'The Tibetan Book of the Dead'. Have you any comments?"

Oh, I get such a heap of people asking about "The Tibetan Book of the Dead," but, quite truly, it is wholly unsuited for Western people because it is a concept, an abstract concept, and one just cannot turn it into a concrete book of instructions. You see, Evans-Wentz was a very good man indeed, but he was a strong Christian and whatever he wrote was greatly coloured by his instinctive aversion to those heathens who had beliefs so different from his own, so he always "tipped the balance" against the heathen. And, again, you cannot translate abstract terms into concrete phrases, that is why there is so much misconception about acupuncture and about much of the Teachings relating to metaphysics. I believe that any person wanting to study the Book of the Dead should first learn Sanskrit!

Anita Kellaway writes to say, "Could you tell us more about the aura and device that could be made to see one's aura? That is very interesting and could be so useful if some intelligent person would use it right. I don't understand why doctors aren't begging you to make one for them."

Well, I have already written quite a lot about the aura, and an aura machine could be made if one had the money and the female models who would be willing to be studied. I have already said, though, that I can get neither! Some people now believe that the Kirlian system is the answer, but I think I had better mention the Kirlian system in another chapter because to my definite knowledge the Kirlian system of photography is just something going in the wrong direction. I know it to be an absolute waste of time.

CHAPTER EIGHT

In the days of long ago when the Century was yet young "Kaiser Bill" stamped along his corridors in the Palace at Berlin thinking of world conquest, thinking of all the wonders he was going to perform.

Trying to conceal his defective arm he gesticulated enormously with the other in an attempt to compensate for his physical deficiencies and deformities. Kaiser Bill was getting ready to go to England to show off the might of the German Navy at a British naval review.

In a dacha on the outskirts of Moscow the Czar of all the Russias twirled his well-waxed moustache and thought of all the wonders that were going to happen in Russia. About him the courtiers were servile, concealing from the great Czar the truth of things as they were in Russia, concealing the truth about the growing unrest of the people, about the starvation of the peasants. The Czar of all the Russias sent his servants scurrying about him for he was going on a long journey all across Europe to England.

In England preparations were being made for an enormous naval review at Spithead. Heads of State were coming to see the review and all the might of the British Navy was going to be paraded before envious eyes.

The streets of London were cobbled. Horses hooves clattered enormously on the rough stone surface, and the iron-rimmed wheels of hansom cabs juddered as they crossed the uneven cobbles, jarring the passengers inside who were suspended in their carriage only by the leather straps at each corner.

The streets of London were lit largely by gas, that new-fangled thing electricity was taking but slow hold on the great metropolis, and cars—well, cars were not yet to be seen except as a rarity of rarities, as a spectacle that would set everyone's head turning.

The great London hospitals were thronged with eager, devoted young men anxious to make a name for themselves in the new fields of medicine. In one great London hospital an ardent young man, Dr. Kilner, studied and studied and went in for research on that strangest of all things which new-fangled electricity would make possible. X-rays.

Late into the nights he laboured trying different arrangements of voltages—electricity provided by the immense Compton dynamos which were then the most wonderful things to appear in the world of electrics—electrics, because the science of electronics was not yet born.

Dr. Kilner studied all manner of strange methods of investigating the human body. He found that if he used immense voltages and extremely small amperages he could project lights from the edges of the human body. He called it testing for the aura. And then he went further in his researches and found that certain arrangements of prisms and lenses aided by filters of special dyes would enable him to see the aura on a nude human body, but the body had to be nude.

One day poor Dr. Kilner was caught examining a nude

woman by the light of the special lamp. No matter that the intruding doctor could see coloured lights in all manner of strange shades on the screen through which Dr. Kilner looked. His research was closed down, he was hauled before the Board of Governors and the Board of Medical Directors, and he was threatened most solemnly that if he ever did research on the human body again, and in that particular field, he would be disbarred, crossed off the British Medical Association register and—who knows?—with his career in shards around him, he might even end up as a labourer or as an occupant of the local workhouse. Dr. Kilner was given the option of getting out of the medical profession or obeying orders and doing research into the dosages of the newly discovered X-ray photographic treatment.

So to mankind's lasting shame one of the great Discoverers was buried in obscurity. Dr. Kilner lapsed into mediocrity and did merely routine things in the world of X-ray. The science of aura research was lost.

The Great War came, the First Great War. X-rays were used for the first time on wounded soldiers. Medical science advanced, but always in the wrong direction, the X-ray machine was not the answer.

The war was won but not by the winner. The loser, Germany, came out of it best of all. First of all, though, people trundled millions of marks along the streets of Germany. Millions of marks were needed to buy even a poor meal. The mark became devalued, there was much trouble in Germany. Russia, too, was in a state of chaos because a new Party had risen, the Communist Party, the Soviet, and they were making wonderful strides in adapting the new knowledge of the West.

In early 1960 and on to the 1970's an author wrote certain things in books on metaphysics which stimulated the interest of the Russians who were always alert for such things. Numbers of this author's books were taken to Russia and studied by avid investigators. Eventually, under State direction, certain researches were carried out in the Universities of Moscow, studies which broke away from what really was the wrong type of research; X-ray was forgotten for a time in Russia and investigators there used high voltages in an attempt to detect the magnetic field of the human body. In Russia there was no problem about nudity, the individual did not matter, everything was subservient to the needs of the State.

In the course of time so-called civilization went its devious way, and there was a man and woman, husband and wife, in Russia who worked together and managed to make a study of many systems which had been tried in the past. Eventually these people, the Kirlians, were able to devise a modern adaptation of an old system, and by this particular system they found that they were able to obtain certain "phenomena" on photographic film.

Now, this does not mean that the Kirlians have succeeded in photographing the human aura. Definitely they have not, because basically their system is so crude that it can be likened to covering a horse-shoe magnet with a piece of paper and on top of the piece of paper sprinkling iron filings so that the lines of magnetic force would be indicated as the iron filings arranged themselves in a pattern dictated by the magnetic influence from the magnet.

All the Kirlians have been able to do is to make more or less clear that there are certain lines of force about everything. But, once again, the Russians claim that the invention is their's although Nikola Tesla, who was born in 1856, made the apparatus which laid the foundation for "Kirlian photography" and our Nikola wasn't a Russian either!

Certain authors have been to Russia and have returned with wonderful tales of the progress which Russian metaphysicians have attained. Some of these authors have written books about the matter, lauding the Russians higher than the heavens and entirely oblivious of the fact that certain authors in the West had already written about such things and could do all that the Russians could do. One author in particular wrote to various lauding persons pointing out these facts but without ever receiving even an acknowledgement. The author sent to some of these people copies of his own books which had been in print long before the Russians "discovered" all the marvels of which they wrote.

Kirlian photography is a false lead just as was X-ray to Dr. Kilner. Kirlian photography is merely a distorted form of corona discharge, it merely shows a certain static electric discharge, or shielding of a discharge, around the human body.

One can have a horse-shoe magnet, or even a bar magnet, and cover it with a piece of paper, and then if one sprinkles iron filings on the paper one can get a form of one dimensional impression of the magnetic field of the magnet, but that does not constitute exact knowledge of the magnet's performance nor of its composition. It is, in fact, just a parlour trick and nothing more. In such a manner the Kirlian system, which is merely a revival of something going back fifty or sixty years, is nothing but a parlour trick which is leading good sound investigators far off the proper track.

Kirlian photography is amusing, it enables one to do parlour tricks with leaves, etc., and even in colour, but then all corona discharges are in colour, are they not?

126

It is such a pity that people nowadays seem to think that anything exotic—and exotic means only foreign—must necessarily be good, better than the home product. There is an old saying which is very true to the effect that no man is a prophet in his own country. So it is that the Kirlian's, who have merely resurrected an old old system, are getting much attention which would not matter in the slightest except that it is sending reputable scientists off the right direction.

The correct form of X-ray which will come in time will not be those miserable shadows that one sees on a piece of thick film. It will, instead, be an exact colour reproduction of inside the human body, and if Dr. Kilner had not been side-tracked he would have produced such a form of photograph because he was on the right trail, he had the knowledge, knowledge which he brought down from the astral, and toward the realization of which he was just fumbling.

Correct X-ray—it would have been called something different at that time, of course—would have enabled doctors and surgeons to see precisely what was happening inside the body and exactly as it was happening and in its own natural colour. Then there would have been no need for exploratory operations, one would have seen instead.

And if those doctors had only listened to Dr. Kilner aura photography also would have been a commonplace, and with photography of the aura one can tell precisely what ailments a body suffers from, and, even more interesting, one can also tell with complete accuracy what ailments a body is likely to suffer from unless remedial steps were taken at an early stage.

Aura photography is very real, it is very necessary to the human race. It was commonplace in the days of Atlantis, it was commonplace when the Sumerians were upon the Earth, and yet—through jealousy, through spite, and through spiritual blindness, researchers with the basic knowledge have been prevented from making such apparatus.

One of the greatest stumbling blocks, it seems, is that a person must be nude to be examined at the aura level, and in hospitals now it is permissible to examine one small area of the human body while the rest is completely draped. It seems to be a crime of some sort to look upon a nude body unless they be on the beach or the stage or in the pages of some of the more pornographic magazines.

But in time X-rays as we know them today will be swept away, gone in to the limbo of forgotten things, gone, too, will be the latest gimmick, Kirlian photography, which if it is ever mentioned as being in the past will be with a condescending smile at the credulity of the stupid people of the 70's who could be taken in by such a gimmick. Kirlian photography, then, is not the answer to aura photography, it is not aura photography at all.

· If you go by the side of a swift flowing river and you put your hand in the water you will find that there are ripples and disturbances of the smooth flow. Your hand has upset the even tenor of the water's flow and made itself manifest by ripples and a wake which spreads outwards. In the same way if one has a very high voltage and a very low amperage connected to certain metal plates and the electricity be switched on, then anything which impedes the flow of that electro-static current will also show as ripples, or speckles, which are merely amusing to look at and have no worthwhile content at all.

Well, I hope that will assist some of you to form your own opinion about Kirlian photography. I have been sickened by the whole affair because I think I must have had the world's largest collection of cuttings about Kirlian photography. People have cut out loads of articles and have sent them on to me. Some of these people, in fact, have such big parcels of cuttings and articles that they felt I should be honoured to pay the postage, so they have sent off these things and I have had to pay double postage on things I knew all about!

That reminds me that some time ago a man in St. Catherine's, Ontario—I think he must have been mental or something—loaded up boxes with the most awful junk of magazines and paperbacks that he could lay his hands on, and he sent them all to me carriage forward! Well, in those days I was younger and more innocent than I am now so I took in those things after paying a very considerable charge for special delivery, special handling, and all the rest of it, and I found that the stuff he had sent me—unsolicited—was muck. But he didn't get away with it; he made one little mistake in which I could see that he had been doing, of which his company would thoroughly disapprove, so I got in touch with the company and sent the evidence to them, and—well, I had a letter of apology and of thanks from the company concerned and *I* had no trouble whatever with that smart Alec who thought he was going to take a rise out of me. But in case anyone else is inclined to send me stuff "collect", save yourself the trouble because I do not accept anything now "collect." I have had people try to telephone me from all over the U.S.A. who thought I was foolish enough to accept collect telephone calls or collect telegrams. Well, they had to think again.

I have also stopped giving my telephone number to people because when I was in Vancouver I found I was getting extraordinarily high telephone bills and I just could not understand what I was being charged for calls to other cities for, and so the matter was investigated. It was found that a near neighbour who knew my telephone number had been giving it to the operator when he was making long distance calls. Nice fellow, eh? Well, he didn't get away with it either.

But now here are some more questions and some more answers. A question here says, "It's five years now since you wrote 'Beyond the Tenth' in which you said that it may be necessary for the Gardeners of the Earth to step in and shake things (humans) up so that we realize what a mess we have made of this planet. Well, things are steadily getting worse, as you said, Communism is spreading rapidly and Unions are gaining what will amount to complete control of many countries fairly soon. In the light of this can you tell us if we are going to get a well deserved kick in the pants within the next thirty or forty years?"

Yes, my friend, but first of all the Gardeners of the Earth do not want to interfere if humans will pick themselves up and put themselves on the right path, because if the Gardeners of the Earth have to come in then there will be drastic measures taken and they don't want that any more than we want it.

In my opinion the world will become Communist just about everywhere, and people will have a very bad time indeed, and not until people have had such a bad time and have shaken themselves out of it will they be able to straighten up and take the upward swing of the pendulum which, in the course of time, will lead to the Golden Age.

I've got a "P.S." here, and it reads, "Can you please explain the relationship and/or difference of hypnosis to meditation, and is hypnosis a worthwhile endeavour for overcoming bad habits or problems?"

Actually there is no relationship at all between meditation and hypnosis. In meditation one is completely under one's own control, able to send one's intellect soaring out to other dimensions. Mind you, I am talking about "meditation," none of that cult nonsense for which one pays a lot of money and gets nothing in return. It is my firm belief that the only meditation worthwhile is that which is done alone because just think of people; everyone has an aura, and the aura can extend quite a way from the body. So if you get a whole bunch of people together then you get auras jamming the meditation processes of others. In my opinion you cannot truly, or satisfactorily, meditate in a group.

In hypnosis one surrenders control to oneself to another person, and I maintain it weakens one's self-control. After all, you want to be YOU, don't you? You don't want to be mixed up with, let us say, Bill Dogsbody. You know what your name is, you know what you are, you know what you would like to be. You like your own privacy, and so why should you possibly want to get hypnotized which is a process under which you surrender part of your privacy to another person? No, I am against hypnotism, dead against it, it is such a harmful thing. You get, for example, a stage hypnotist who says that he will cure a certain person of a certain complaint. Well, he doesn't do that. If he is a hypnotist he can, undoubtedly, influence the person to hide or disguise the symptoms of the illness, and then if the symptoms are disguised how can one expect that even the most intelligent doctor will find out that from which the person suffers? By the time the victim has been hypnotized for a certain period then the illness usually is quite incurable.

131

So my strong advice is—never allow yourself to be hypnotized unless it is by a fully qualified medical practitioner who has also been trained in hypnotic practices and techniques. As a doctor he will have taken note of your symptoms, as a hypnotist he will know how to channel those symptoms into any worthwhile path possible. Remember that a doctor takes an oath to give one relief from pain and to do no evil!

Well, our friend Mr. John Bigras and the two Bigras cats have gone roaring off to Banff and on to Vancouver. I have been out twice since coming from hospital, two little visits to the outskirts of the city, two little trips when I could look out over the city from the foothills leading to the Rockies. Now, I suppose, once again I am a "shut-in", stuck here mainly in one room in a bed or in a wheelchair. Cars are very useful things, but I do not have one. Anyway, they are far too expensive on an author's income, as I told the Income Tax people when they tried to deny me an income tax allowance on the purchase of an electric wheelchair. Well, one doesn't have a wheelchair for pleasure but only because it is essential. I told them that with my disabilities I should really be on Welfare, instead of that I work at writing books to make myself independent of Welfare. But instead of the Income Tax people giving me any concessions they try to deduct the last penny they can. For instance, I paid my income tax and then from one department I got a note saying that my income tax was all clear. The very next day I got another note from another department saying I had to pay a fine because I paid my tax once a year instead of every three to six months. So people who work as brick-layers or navvies or cab drivers or anything like that are far better off tax-wise than I am because the Income Tax people soak me the limit and beyond, and I often wonder at the mentality and personality of these people who can be income tax collectors and batten on the troubles of disabled people. However, that is not answering questions, is it, and that is what this book is supposed to be. So let's get on with the unending pile of questions. They grow, you know! I have enough questions here for ten or twenty books, and yesterday I had a whole bunch of quite abstract metaphysical questions sent on from Brasil.

"Is it important enough for the inhabitants of this plane to know more of the other planes of existence beyond the astral? If so, could you elucidate on them, perhaps give us at least a sketchy idea of the structure of the planes of existence? Also, what happens when a spirit evolves to the plane 'below' that of the highest, or that of God? Can a spirit actually evolve to the highest plane, or is that too preposterous to even discuss?"

Well, it is only possible to discuss the plane above, the astral, and it is much like this world although it has another dimension. Time, for instance, is not at all the same as it is on this world. Travel is different, too; if you want to get to a place you think yourself there. You might be sitting down looking out across the landscape and feel that you would like to call on a friend who might be a certain distance away. Well, if you think of the friend, and think of his location, then almost imperceptibly you will find yourself there with your friend.

Nor will you find, in the astral world, prudishness or pornography. When you get to the astral world you find —to your considerable astonishment at first—that you are as bare as a peeled banana and you have quite literally to "think up" any form of clothing which takes your fancy. But after a time—well, you find that these things do not

133

matter, the things of the spirit count more, and that is not as a pun either!

In the astral plane you cannot meet people with whom you are antagonistic, and of course the higher you go the more compatible you are with the people around you.

Now, you can usually get up to about the ninth plane of existence and then you no longer find that the Overself is sending out puppets. Instead there is only one extension from the Overself, after the ninth plane.

Of course there are a vast number of planes of existence, and you go on and on getting more and more dimensions, but there would be no point in trying to discuss some of these other dimensions unless you have been there because there is no point of reference. How would you, for example, discuss atomic theory with an ant who was more interested in getting on with the ordinary business of day to day living? How could you discuss nuclear thermo electrics with a bee who was far more interested in going out and collecting pollen, or whatever they collect, so that the process of making honey could continue? No, until you have had experience of other dimensions you are not able to discuss them. It's like having a year old baby trying to discuss brain surgery with one of our leading surgeons.

But there is no limit to how high you can go. Remember the old saying that there is always plenty of room at the top of the ladder. And, you see, God is not an old gent with a beard and a shepherd's crook who comes along and hooks in all the wayward lambs. God is a different thing altogether, nothing that you can understand down here. Here your nearest conception of a God is a Manu, that is, one of the Branch Managers who looks after this particular departmental store which we call Earth. Under him he has a lot of Assistant Managers who look after continents, lands, and cities. They seem to have made a pretty poor show of it of late, don't they? Think of all the commotion in America, in Cambodia, in Viet-Nam, in the Middle East, and now in Cyprus. I think all these Manus should be sent back to take a special post graduate course or something.

But anyway, that is getting away from the subject. So the answer is that you can go as high as your capacity will allow, and there is no reason at all why you should not reach the top and reach "Buddhahood", that is what Buddhism is about, anyway.

"Can we of this physical plane learn of and effectively use astrology for the good of the living? If so, what is the true source of astrological teachings?"

Many, many years ago astrology was extraordinarily accurate because it was founded on a new science, the influence of the stars on objects of this Earth—humans, animals, plants, etc.—had been predicated, and those assumptions were accurate so long as the zodiac remained as it was when the assumptions were made.

Now, a few thousand years later, the zodiac is different and the predictions, the forecasts are all wrong. I personally believe that astrology as it is in the West nowadays is just a waste of time, it is utterly inaccurate for the simple reason that no allowance has been made for the difference in the configuration of the zodiac. In the very Far East such allowances have been made and the horoscopes there are very very much more accurate. I know this; everything that was predicted for me by astrologers in the very Far East has come true—every darn thing!

I have had my horoscope done several times in the West and each time the predictions could hardly have been more incorrect, they might have been doing a horoscope for a different person, their efforts have proved to be ludicrous. So I always tell people that in my considered opinion, and based on my own experience with astrologers in the West, it is just a waste of time to have one's horoscope done.

People are always writing to me asking that I should do their horoscopes "and at least one incarnation," and I always refuse because to do a horoscope properly takes a very considerable time and I do not have that time. I have been offered quite remarkable sums of money to do a horoscope, but I always without exception refuse.

People seem vastly interested in getting "at least one incarnation" told, but why? If people are on this Earth now living through this life now, what does it matter what they were in the past? All that matters is what they are now and what they are going to be in the future, and if a person just squanders time thinking about the glories of the past, etc., etc., ad lib, then they end up with a chip on their shoulder and think "Oh, I was Cleopatra's grandmother in the last life and now look at me—what am I, a cleaning lady!"

Hey! I like this one:—

"Do you have an opinion on the martial arts? Is it possible for Americans to study the form of Judo, Karate, or whatever the martial form was that you were taught in Tibet?"

In the Far East the martial arts—so called—were not for the purpose of disabling people nor were they for defence. They were, instead, designed as a mental, mystical, and spiritual discipline. After all, the more colourful you are the more your conscience tells you to be gentle, the more you have been trained about the body the more you can look after your own body. So people who think they are going to take a correspondence course in Judo, for instance, and then beat up the bully who kicks sand at them when they are on the beach—well, they are in for a shock. For instance, I do not think that these arts can be taught properly by correspondence, nor by any young punk who thinks he is going to set up a physical training school. There is more to it than that, there is always the danger, too, that you try to disable someone who is perhaps ten or twenty lessons ahead of you, as I have stated previously in this book! You could indeed "collect your lumps" that way. So my own recommendation is that going in for this martial art stunt is useless if you want it just for defence. No Judo or Karate is useful against a gun, is it? Especially when the bullet is already speeding toward you.

Well, Kathi Porter, I will answer your questions—sorry, I have already answered some of them—but I will answer another. It is, "Is it wise to pray to our Overself for direction or guidance and that things, mainly of the occult and spiritual, be revealed to us as we can accept and understand them?"

Yes, Kathi, you can always pray to your Overself. Your Overself knows everything that has ever happened to the Overself. But look at it like this; you are employed here in (where shall we say?) America, and your Big Boss is living in—oh, let's say Sydney, Australia. Now, if you want to get in touch with your Boss you have to use a letter or a telephone. Let's cut out the letter because you can't send a letter to your Overself, and your Big Boss is the equivalent of your Overself. So that leaves us with a telephone, and if you have ever tried to telephone half way across the world you will have discovered that it is a frustrating, time wasting, patience consuming experience. And then half the words you might have to guess.

Your sub-conscious is like a Librarian. The Librarian doesn't need to know much herself, her chief value is in that she knows where to find certain information. So a Librarian can be consulted about any problem, and if she is a good Librarian she can tell you just where to look, what type of book will give the information that you need. She will also tell you where the book is on the Library shelves. The sub-conscious is like that, the sub-conscious is a pretty dim sort of individual, but he or she knows exactly how to get the information you want so if you get in touch with your sub-conscious you will find you get results far more quickly than if you waste energy trying to contact your Overself. It is much quicker to look up a thing in your local library than to telephone somebody in Australia or Timbuktoo or Tuscaloosa, or somewhere else.

There is a very modest lady who lives in Barcelona, Spain. She has some questions but she prefers not to have her name mentioned. So I will just give my greetings to Senora D. and answer some questions from her:—

"Are the forerunners of the New World Leader already making propaganda or preparing for him?"

Even according to the Christian Bibles this is a time (Revelations) when there shall be false prophets. In other words, translated into modern day language, this poor old world of ours is in a horrible mess, all the standards and values are tumbling down around us, and there is always some smart Alec ready to make a fast buck by pretending to be a World Leader. So it is we sometimes find that some people with ample money will sponsor a young punk and pretend that he is the new Messiah or the new God or something else, and these moneyed men who hunger more and more for more and more money will put on quite a show with all the theatrical trappings, jet planes, fast cars, etc., trying to delude the unwary or the ignorant into paying money to join a special movement. After a time the young punk grows up a bit and he wants a say in his own affairs, and unless the moneyed people can control him he does things which his followers find incompatible with his professed aims.

Sometimes, too, the fellow goes to another country and the tax collectors of the country seize a few of his millions or won't let him out of the country until he does pay a few millions. Sometimes a fellow will go around and find that his aircraft has been seized because it wasn't his and it had been taken out of the country.

My own strong, strong recommendation is that no one be taken in by these cultists, these advertising people who claim that they and they only are the true God, the new Messiah, the new Leader, the Guru of all Gurus, etc. You want to look behind the facade and ask yourself— well, what are these people getting out of it, why all the big advertisements? If they were genuine they wouldn't need to advertise, people would still KNOW and would come flocking to the holy banner.

Cults? Those who form cults are, in my opinion, the scum of the Earth because they lead away the gullible and deny them a chance of really getting knowledge.

Hey, getting fierce, aren't I? You didn't know I could be fierce in my old age, did you? Never mind, it's a good thing to let off steam sometimes because if I can shock some of you into staying away from the cults then it will be to the good of your own spiritual health.

"It is a shame that we don't know more about those extraordinary men, the Lama Mingyar Dondup and the Great Thirteenth Dalai Lama."

The Lama Mingyar Dondup is, indeed, a Great Entity who is now, of course, far beyond the Earth sphere. He is not incarnated but is, instead, on a much higher plane of existence and he is actually trying to help other worlds—

139

worlds, plural—he is not concentrating solely on this Earth but on a whole group of inhabited worlds where they are having trouble, where selfishness is growing like weeds in a garden.

Some of us true Lamas believe that the Great Thirteenth was the last of the Dalai Lamas. We believe that if the present encumbent to that office had been a true Dalai Lama he would have done more to help the people of Tibet. After all, when a man just says he is a religious leader and he is praying—well, anyone can pray. It needs more than a few prayers to free a country from Communist aggressors, Communist invaders, it needs an actual physical example. It might even mean martyrdom for a leader of a country, because if a leader of a country stays and fights with his people—and sometimes force is justified—then his people will not be faint-hearted when they have a well-loved leader to lead them. The Great Thirteenth was such a man, one who would have stayed with his people, but you can't fight against death, can you?

CHAPTER NINE

I have just had my very meagre meal, and that reminds me of a question which arrived only yesterday—barely in time for this book, is it, because it's going ahead. Anyway, I had a letter yesterday, "Please write another book!!!!! And please put in something about fasting. What do you think about fasting? Should people fast? What harm can it cause anyway?"

140

So I can only reply—Glory be, missus, I've been fasting for years! Seriously, though, fasting—with brains—is a very good thing indeed provided you take some commonsense precautions. For example, you don't go fasting if you are diabetic, you don't go fasting if you've got certain types of heart disease. But if you are in average good health then it really does help to fast at times provided you don't have to do a full day's work at the same time.

You would not have an automobile and expect it to work if the fuel tank was empty, so why should you expect your own human body to work when there is no feed left for it to draw upon?

Normally it is perfectly safe to fast when you have a vacation because when you have a vacation you can rest more, you do not have to run for the bus, you do not have to put on an extra spurt of work when the boss glances in your direction, you can do it in your own time. So if you are going to fast make sure that you are in reasonably good health and do not have any of those diseases or complaints such as diabetes because you can upset yourself by fasting if you are diabetic. Assured on these points, then you should make sure that your internal plumbing is in good order and that you are not suffering from hold-up in the rear delivery department. You should take a mild laxative so that you are fairly empty inside. Then you stop eating, but you do not stop drinking. If you are fasting you would be well advised to take anything which the medical profession calls a clear liquid diet. Plenty of water, fruit juices, but nothing of a solid nature whatever, not even milk because milk is too solid for this purpose.

Now, do not think that you are going to fast and suck candies. That is not fasting, that is cheating, that is making the whole thing a farce. So stop eating, do quite a bit of resting. You can read, listen to radio or watch TV, but no gallivanting off to the cinema or to the pub or to anything of that nature. If you do you will deplete your fat resources faster than will be comfortable. You see, if you are going to fast your body has got to keep on working and the only way it can keep on working is to gradually absorb the stored up food in your body cells, that means in your fat cells, and if you go racing around going out on social occasions or doing manual work then you will lose weight too quickly and will definitely risk collapse.

To give you an idea of what I am talking about let me tell you that of late there have been an astonishing number of really obese people who have had an operation to short-circuit perhaps six or ten feet of their intenstines so they do not absorb their food so much. If too much of the intestine has been short-circuited then the person loses weight too rapidly and all sorts of strange things happen. There was one woman weighing over three hundred pounds, I think she weighed about three hundred and fifty pounds, actually, and she had ten feet of intestine short-circuited. She was moaning and groaning with dismay because she lost weight so rapidly that she felt dreadfully ill most of the time and her flesh was draped about her in folds, which is not a good thing for a lady who has some pride in her appearance.

Go carefully, then, if you are going to fast. Stop eating and stop working, rest a lot, and by "rest" it is meant that you should not go out and do shopping or go to entertainments. If you want to fast and get all the benefits of fasting without any of the drawbacks you will have to forego not merely food but mobility.

You need a lot of fluid otherwise you will become dehydrated, and if you are dehydrated you will affect your health very badly. It is a horrible thing to happen to one.

Certain people with poor health find that if they do fast their liver becomes affected, so make sure that your health is good enough before you go in for any of these things like fasting.

How long should you fast? Well, until you start seeing things, if you like. You can go four or five days without food with much good result. Before I went into hospital this last time I was without any food at all for just over ten days, and when I got in the hospital I was without food for a few more days! It didn't do me any harm. So you can only say that you fast so long as you feel the need to fast. You should not fast more than four or five days without taking the advice of your doctor, and if he is the ordinary crummy type of fellow who can see no further than his medical text books he will tell you straight out that you are crazy to fast, but that is because he's never done it. But, for your own protection, you should always get medical advice if you are going to fast for more than four or five days.

When you start to eat after—well, don't just gulp down half a cow or you will have all sorts of troubles, indigestion and all the rest of it, and very bad indigestion it will be.

When you are fasting your stomach shrinks. It shrinks to the size of a small egg because there is no reason why it should be distended if you are not taking in food. Well, after five days or so your stomach is the size of a small egg, and it has become used to being that size, so if you suddenly get sick of fasting and cram down a whole load of stuff then your stomach will have to distend far more than it likes doing so you will get pain, and your intestines will have shrunk through having no material inside and the intestines, too, will have to stretch enormously. Believe me, if you go and gormandize after five days of fasting you will get more aches and pains than you thought possible from such a simple thing.

After a fast take very light meals, milk and a few biscuits. Next day take a bit more. But do not go back to your normal food intake until about three or four days after. In that way you will get good results from your fast, but contrariwise, if you go and stuff after a fast you will get all harm which will make your fast useless.

Now here is something I am going to tell you. I've got a letter here and the writer says, "I have several times attempted to visit you in the astral. I always see 'some-one' who slightly resembles you but who is quite weird indeed. The person always attempts to play the part of you, but they are quite poor actors. Perhaps you are too busy doing other things in other worlds to be seen. Perhaps before this letter is completed you might be visited by me, even though I am still in the prehistoric stage of astral travelling."

My dear madam, I am delighted to tell you that I have an effective barrier so that people cannot visit me in the astral unless I want them to. You see, I get lots of people —literally lots—who tell me they are going to visit me in the astral, and if they all could do so then I should have no privacy, I should have no time to myself, and—would YOU like a crowd of people visiting you when you were in the bath, for example? I do not! So through knowledge which was given to me many many years ago I have been able to make a barrier which means that I cannot be visited by any Earth person unless I am willing to be so visited.

You have seen mischievous entities such as people see

at seances. I have written about this before so there is no point in going into it in detail, but quite a lot of people in the "tween worlds" want to be humans, they are entities now, bundles of life force without much sentient thought, in fact, as I have already said, they are like mischievous monkeys. And if a person tries to visit me and I don't want to see them then one of these mischievous entities will move in and pretend to be me. So if people try to visit me they've only got themselves to blame!

People send me all manner of demands that I should visit them. Some send me intricately marked maps or photographs showing precisely where they live and they command me to appear at such-and-such a time. Well, of course, I do no such thing. Would you go flitting about in the astral just because some creep who has paid a few pence for a book thinks he or she has the right to dictate to the author? Pox to them, is what I say!

There are only twenty-four hours in the day, and if I did obey these imperious demands I should need thirty hours at least. Furthermore, these people have no conception of the difference in time. I live in a mountain time zone, but what about a person in Tokyo demanding my presence? There is quite a lot of difference in time, in fact it is the next day. So why should I bother to work out what time it is in that other location or what day it is? No, people who demand—who command—my presence as though I were a slave of a lamp or something else, they've got another think coming. They might even have two thinks coming!

It's quite amusing, too, because sometimes I get demands from people that I should instantly appear and find a pen which they have mislaid or a ring or a letter. Oh yes, I am perfectly sincere in that; I had a most imperial command just a short time ago—a person had put down something and couldn't find it, and she wanted it to wear that night so she thought she could will me to come and I would instantly appear on the spot and produce the goods for her. Well, I think she should go back to reading Aladdin and his magic lamp, don't you? Or perhaps she should grow up instead.

Here is something I am sure will make you laugh. I will copy it out for you now:—

"Last night when I was astral travelling I decided to go on a teaching spree. Suddenly as I was walking along I noticed I had a BEAUTIFUL ORANGE SAFFRON ROBE on. I was so thrilled! Astral clothes are so beautiful. I had decided I was going to teach some people when suddenly as I was walking along the saffron robe disappeared and I was stark naked. My mind went blank, the last thing I remember is standing naked in the middle of a public building without any clothes on!"

Yes, that's what happens, you see. People go into these things without any preparation. This person did indeed get into the astral but forgot to keep a corner of the mind—astral mind—continually on her clothing, so as soon as she decided that she was going to teach some people who already knew more than she did, the little bit of her mind which should have been dealing with clothes switched off, and then—well, she was embarrassed standing in the middle of this public building with, no doubt, quite a crowd of interested on-lookers. Well, wouldn't YOU be interested as well if you suddenly saw a woman appear naked in front of you? The streakers nowadays seem to attract a lot of attention so you judge for yourself what your reactions would be.

This particular person wants me to mention her by name, but unfortunately I can't even read her name, and I can't read her address either because she didn't give any. So I can only refer to her as The Nameless One. She also wants to know when will flying saucers start coming in great numbers. Well, actually, I shall be surprised if there are not more reports of flying saucers in the immediate future, and I am going to suggest something to you—just think of this; you will have read from time to time that naval ships of Norway, Denmark, Sweden or somewhere else have bottled up a "submarine" in one of the fjords, and there is no possible way for it to escape. Fine, we read all about that, we hear all about it on the radio, and we are convinced that this unknown submarine which, it is hinted, must obviously be Russian is bottled up, it cannot escape. Warships of the United Nations are there in force with all their submarine detection gear and they are ready to blow the submarine straight out of the water if it doesn't surrender. You've read about that in the newspapers, haven't you? You've heard it on the radio, haven't you? All right, now think of this; did you ever hear of any result? Did you? I think you did not because everything is hushed-up, and I have reason to believe that there are U.F.O.'s which come from inside the Earth and which are able to navigate under water just as submarines do, and I believe that these U.F.O.'s are sometimes detected by ships of different nations, but these U.F.O.'s can always escape.

There was a prediction made many many years ago to the effect that this year, 1974, there would be a confrontation between ships of the world and a U.F.O. under the water. The prediction is to the effect that there would be a collision between a submarine and a U.F.O., and some of the U.F.O. people would be rescued and then it would be seen quite clearly that they were not humans as the term is understood on the surface of the Earth. Predictions could be a little time out, you know, so I really think something like that will happen in 1974 or 1975 IF IT HAS NOT ALREADY HAPPENED.

I say, "if it has not already happened" because it seems so strange to me that things are hushed up so much by Governments. We hear that a submarine has been trapped, much commotion is caused, many reports are given, almost hour by hour reports, and then suddenly ... nothing, nothing more is said, everything is forgotten. No matter what enquiries are made, no one knows anything about it any more, it's just as if it did not happen. Now, if some aliens had been found and possibly rescued from a U.F.O. then, of course, the Governments would step in and conceal all the knowledge from those who have a right to know—the people—until the Governments concerned decided how the knowledge could be best turned to the advantage of the Governments concerned.

Here is another nice question, "Under what conditions can you gain access to the Akashic Records to find out another person's future?"

You cannot if you are a normal human without very very special life-time training. The Akashic Record of each person is closed and cannot be seen by any other human (normally) until the subject of that Record leaves the Earth and is in the Hall of Memories where the poor wretch has to see it all and blush alarmingly with shame!

I think this particular correspondent should go to a good eye specialist because he writes, "Dr. Rampa, did you know that you have an amazing resemblance to King Feisal of Saudi Arabia? Yes, quite definitely I state that there was a picture of King Feisal on a Time magazine, and you look just like him."

King Feisal, Your Majesty, may I offer you my humble apologies because if you look like me—well, you sure have got a load on you! Personally I don't see any resemblance except that King Feisal has two eyes, one nose, one mouth and two ears. Yes, I have just that, two eyes, one nose, one mouth and two ears, oh yes, then of course there must be a resemblance. But then I think King Feisal has a lot more hair than I have, I am bald, in fact the flies use the top of my head as a skating rink in hot weather.

"Is it possible to have a physical or astral child as a result of astral intercourse?"

No, not a chance, although to believe some of my correspondents it not merely is possible but it does occur. For example, when I was living at Prescott, Ontario, many years ago I had a woman write to me—I have never seen her, never been closer to her than a few hundred miles—and she told me that she was now pregnant by me and she was going to bear my child. According to her, I visited her in the astral and (let me be delicate) "gave her the works." Well, that was certainly news to me, I seem to have missed all the fun because I certainly don't know anything about it. The poor lady didn't seem to realize that the husband with whom she sleeps and with whom she presumably does other things may have been more responsible than I was. But, anyway, I will tell you—no, it is not possible to go round in the astral impregnating women. Sorry to spoil your fun but there it is, you can't do it.

Now this is a good question, it is, "Sometimes I see small children who seem to be talking to themselves but who are really talking to 'someone.' They usually stare as if they are looking directly at someone I can't see, they sometimes carry on long conversations. Who are they talking to? Nature Spirits? Also, can little children see into the astral world at any time they wish?"

Of course these children are able to talk and see people

in the astral. It is a simple matter indeed because when a child is small their vibrations are higher, and so they can get in touch with people in the astral whose vibrations are lower. There are also special spirit friends who look after children, in other words, fairies are real, and not until stupid parents tell children that they mustn't tell lies and of course they don't see other people do the children lose the ability. In fact parents are a child's worst friends. Parents too often think that they are omnipotent, the source of all knowledge. They try to dominate their children and they crush out and ruin natural abilities of the child. It is a very sad thing, it is adults who make it so difficult for astral people to contact this world.

Do you want to smile? Well, what would you answer to a question like this:—"Why can't Buddhist monks get married?"

Let me answer that with a question. The question is, "Why cannot Catholic priests get married?" Obviously because it is a facet of the religion, of the religious discipline. Many churches, not merely Christian churches, either, think that a man must devote his whole life to that religion. He must, in effect, marry the religion. Many churches, or many religions, believe that if a man marries then his mind might be on other things—the attractions of his wife, for instance—and he would then not be able to give full time attention to his religious duties. That is why Catholics and some other priests do not marry. But there are many Buddhist monks of different sects who do marry, just as there are many different types of Christian priest who do marry. Protestant priests marry, Catholic priests do not. It's just a matter of belief and that is all there is to it.

I have a regular correspondence with a lady and gentleman who have a son who has a mental defect. The son is retarded. Unfortunately medical science does not seem able to do much for such people, and often they try to persuade the parents of such a child to commit the child to some Home for the Mentally Defective.

This particular boy is improving, and I believe that in time, with the loving care of his parents, he will become very much more normal. It seems that when he was a baby a doctor treated him unwisely and tried out a new drug on the small baby giving it a dosage which would have overpowered a strong adult. From that time on the boy has suffered very great mental strain and he cannot speak, and I believe that his mental health is improving. I have suggested that he be sent to friends on a farm because often if such a person is mixing with animals, etc., who are less privileged than he, then a great improvement takes place as the boy or girl does all he can, or all she can, to help and to understand the animals.

In many cases a retarded child, seeing an animal, gets a type of fellow feeling. The child thinks that the animal cannot talk either, so that gives him a bond, and when such a child is given the run of a farm and given tasks within his or her capabilities, then the responsibility does start up and spark a response in the intelligence.

It is such a shame, such a crime to just rush retarded people off to a mental home when there is any hope at all that kindness at home, or kindness and understanding on a farm, will enable the retarded one to become less retarded. I have known many cases where Mongolian idiots —they are not idiots by any means—have been greatly improved by being placed in a position where they can help with animal husbandry.

Do you remember in a previous book that I made a prediction that a President of the U.S.A. would be removed from office? Well, as I write this we are waiting for President Nixon to announce his resignation. The poor fellow has had enough pressure, certainly, and according to what one reads in the papers he is certainly having some nervous strain which may have affected his mental health. But anyway—predictions sometimes come right, you know. But I have been told quite reliably that President Nixon—probably former President when you read this—was informed by a quite well-known woman astrologer or whatever she is that nothing would happen to him. Well, she wasn't very successful, was she?

Actually, everything comes in cycles. You get troubles with Kings, Presidents and all the rest of it in certain cycles. So if you know where to look you can find out about these periodic cycles. In the same way you can find out fairly accurately when a next war is going to happen. If you had been sufficiently interested to work out the dates of wars and you had drawn a graph of them, you would have found that they follow a more or less regular pattern. Everything happens like that, you know. Even with human life everything happens in cycles as every woman knows, and then there are the cycles of the Moon's phases. But in addition to that there are the cycles which affect humans most of all, such as the twenty-three day cycle of up's and down's of health, and the twenty-eight day cycle, and another cycle which occurs over a period of thirty-three days. We get the health, the nervous energy, and the intellect, all fluctuating from top to bottom. And obviously as the three cycles come together at fairly long intervals then one can have an extremely good period for a day or so, or an extremely bad period for a day or so.

I keep a regular chart of my cycles, that is, the twenty-three day, the twenty-eight day, and the thirty-three day cycles, and quite recently I was at a peak of what passes for good health with me, as was predicted by the three cycles. But then there came the decline of the three cycles all in a bunch, and the result of that was that I was carted off to hospital, a very sick fellow indeed with more pain than I like to think about. Then I stayed in the hospital until the cycles changed around and permitted me to feel better, after which I came out again.

All life has cycles of this type, and if you know how they can be charted. Not only that, but if you know how you can find out the cycles of world events, what's going to happen to this country, what's going to happen to that, what sort of person is going to be assassinated next, and what those naughty little Russian lads are going to do to upset the equanimity of the world. It is a pity that the Russians are so xenophobic because they make a lot of misery for themselves always being absolutely positive that everyone else is against the poor little Russians, whereas actually most of the time people couldn't care two hoots for the Russians. They play pretty rough, though, as I know to my cost.

Would it not be a very pleasant thing if we could get our Lords and Masters, who pose as a democratic elected Government, to prepare proper charts showing world events and when we can expect an increase in income tax, or—oh wonderful event!—a decrease in income tax, although the latter doesn't seem possible. The Governments are always willing to put up the prices, to increase the taxes, etc., but they never do a darn thing about reducing them, do they? The income tax thing, I believe it came under one of the terms of the Defence of the Realm Act (D.O.R.A.) in England during the 1914–1918 war, was just a temporary measure which was going to be repealed at the end of the war. Well, now, here in Canada as well as in the U.S.A., the Government of the country imposes a whacking great tax, and then the Province or State take their bite was well by imposing a big tax, and in some places there is a third income tax, that which is imposed by a money-hungry city. It reminds me of the sort of life an author lives; first of all he pays commission to one or two agents, and then he pays income tax in the country which is publishing a book, and then he loses money on the rate of exchange—it's never in my favour!—and then he's got to pay tax, poor fellow, in his own country. And if he is particularly unlucky he has to pay Federal tax and then Provincial tax, and if this is not "his day" he has to pay city tax as well. After that he may find that there is some sort of a school tax because the Catholics, for some strange reason, seem to have twisted the arm of the Governments so they can dun money out of people to help pay for the schooling of little Catholics. It's a strange, strange world, isn't it?

But my Respected Friend, Paddle Boat Moffet, has a question; Paddle Boat loves ships, and because of his love of ships I renamed him "Paddle Boat", a name which it seems he thoroughly enjoys. Paddle Boat Moffet is a very gifted model maker. To my disgust he has been making silly old sailing ship models of an age long past. After all, who wants to know about ships which are mere lumps of wood blown along by a bit of cloth stuck on to a bit of a stick called a mast? All the best modellers make paddle boat models or good old steam ships, and so—Paddle Boat Moffet, fired by his new name, is now busy making a paddle boat.

But he is puzzled about the Marie Celeste. You probably all know about her, but if there is Aunt Agatha out there who doesn't know let me tell you, auntie, that the Marie Celeste is, or was, a sailing ship which was plying her regular route across the seas, and then one day, or rather, one evening, an oncoming ship saw the Marie Celeste coming toward her with all sails set, booming along in front of the wind. But—like this book—it was twilight, and according to marine law the Marie Celeste should have had lights showing but there were no lights, and the people aboard the oncoming ship were perturbed at several things which seemed wrong with the Marie Celeste. So after quite a long chase some of the men from the spectator ship were able to board the Marie Celeste and lower the sails.

Then they got gooseflesh, or whatever it is that seamen get when they are scared stiff, because there was no one aboard the Marie Celeste, no one at all, everything was perfectly in order, even a meal was laid out on a table waiting for an unknown diner.

Throughout years and years many conjectures have been made as to what happened aboard the Marie Celeste. There was no sign whatever of any violence, so—what could it have been? The life-boats were there so the crew could not have taken off from what they thought was a sinking ship. The ship was perfectly in order, nothing at all wrong with it, except . . . the crew were not aboard, and that is all.

There have been quite a lot of ships like that. The ships have been intact in perfect order, and yet there has been no one aboard. And then if you will read my other books you will read about the Bermuda Triangle in which not only ships have lost their crews, but the ships themselves have disappeared. Aircraft have disappeared as well, and in at least one authenticated case voices were heard on the radio fading out in eerie, ghostly fashion.

Paddle Boat Moffet wants to know what happened.

Well, there is another time-dimension which crosses our world. There is another world intermingled with ours. A lot of people say, "Well, if that is so why can't we see it?" You cannot because it is on a different frequency. Think of it like this; I don't know how many of you are interested in short-wave radio but quite a number of you will have had the acquaintance of listening to a short-wave station—oh, let's say just for example, the B.B.C. on the 31 meter band, and then find that the station appeared to drift off and instead there would be perhaps Moscow, the Voice of Moscow bellowing out propaganda against the Capitalist countries. And then, even before one could reach for the tuning knob, the drift would occur again, bawling Moscow would disappear and the B.B.C. would come back. All the time, of course, both stations were broadcasting, but the set was tuned to one, and if there was a frequency drift somewhere the other would come in instead. We get the same thing with the two worlds. The worlds are invisible to each other.

Let me put it in another way; we here on this world see by a certain type of light, but supposing our light was switched off and something else, perhaps infra-red, was switched on then we would apparently be in darkness, but a person who could see by infra-red light would be able to see perfectly whereas he would not be able to see at all by our light. So it is that in such a case if our world is at one frequency and our twin world is at another frequency there is no interaction between them so one world is not aware of another, but in (by way of illustration only) the two worlds intermingling at the Bermuda Triangle particularly, and then there is a drift, any poor soul at the point of the drift would possibly find that he had slipped from one world into the other! He would get a nasty shock, wouldn't he? The other world is a twin of this world, so when he had sailed or flown over the barrier and into this other world he would be in a similar

156

type of world and in a similar location on that world, but he wouldn't know the language, he might not even see so well, he might find that he was seeing almost as one would see at twilight—hey, I can't get away from that word, can I?

But you can rest assured that people from the other world come to this one as well. In fact I know of a definite authentic case where it happened in Argentina because I was near at the time. But that is another story.

So, Paddle Boat Moffet, the Marie Celeste and other ships could still sail if they went over the border, but it might even be that in the case of the Marie Celeste the crew were taken off for examination by a U.F.O., or even by another ship which was on the other side of the "barrier." Either is possible, and both have happened in the case of other ships.

CHAPTER TEN

I have been listening to the tragedy of a nation, using my little old transistor radio, and I am just overcome by the tragedy of it all. Of course by the time you read this book the news will be old, possibly even the new President will have left. I should never be surprised nowadays. But—I have been listening to the tragedy of a nation. The tragedy is not the doings of Richard Nixon. Richard Nixon, I would say, is no saint, in fact I should imagine that he can grow horns on his head far more easily than he would grow wings on his shoulders, but Richard Nixon has done a lot of good, and to my way of thinking he has done no more harm than some of the other people who have been Presidents of the U.S.A.

The tragedy of the U.S.A. is not the tragedy of the President, the tragedy is that the press, those evil dastardly men of the press, have caused all the trouble, and I cannot understand why presumably sane people tolerate the press. There should definitely be a press censorship, but to be crude about it none of the politicos have the guts to impose it or even to suggest it.

I well know how the lying press can fabricate the "evidence," and then the press will accuse a person, try him, and condemn him without one iota of real guilt on the person concerned.

I am not saying that President Nixon was innocent, not even the most potent of those wonderful cleaning powders which are so freely advertised would make President Nixon snow white, no matter how many times he was dunked in the stuff, but he was not as bad as he was painted by the press, and I will go so far as to say that he has not done anything worse than any other President has done. I thoroughly understand President Nixon's point of view, and I should class him as a perfectly ordinary commonplace in-the-rut American President.

The press have no right to interfere in politics any more than the churches have. It is always a source of amazement to me that in Ireland, for example, one bible-thumper has left his lectern, or flown the pulpit, to become one of the revolutionaries. What's the fellow's name? Paisley, I believe. But if a man goes in for Holy Orders why does he suddenly start giving revolutionary orders?

You get the same thing with old Makarios who ran so fast from Cyprus that no one could catch him. He is another one, this time an Archbishop, and he forgot his holy teachings to enter the revolutionary path, and revolutionaries it seems to me, are nothing but a gang of murderers. We are all entitled to our opinions, and that is my opinion. I think that a cleric who forgets his holy teaching and runs bleating from his flock to pick up a rifle should be unfrocked. Not merely should he be unfrocked, he should be debagged. Debag is a good old English term, so for the American audience let me say that he should be peeled from inside his pants!

I have had a lot of persecution by the press, and although I cannot truly say I hate anyone I am as near hating the press as I am anyone in the world. I would prefer to shake hands with Satan and his grandmother—does Satan have a grandmother?—than I would to shake hands with a pressman because these people are truly the scum of the Earth. One listens to them on the radio and one shudders at the arrogant way in which they dictate to people, shudders at the manner in which they try to force a person to say what the pressman wants them to say. And then in the matter of the new incumbent, Gerald Ford, I listened to the pressmen saying what the new President would do. Well, if the press people are so important, so all-knowing, then why does America need a President? Why doesn't the Senate or Congress or the Boy Scouts or something just phone the press each morning to know what orders they should give? The press people, it seems to me, are just a lot of illiterate, ignorant fools who are just ready to cash-in on anyone's misery, and even on a nation's tragedy. Pox to the press!

I have a letter from a person who cannot understand this:—

"Well, in your books, and in other books too, it is said that every so often the world undergoes a sort of change of cycles, a change of civilization, but if that is so then

159

there must be remnants of other civilizations and we never find any, so it leads me to think that you are not telling the truth. It leads me to the belief that the Bible is right and the world is only about three or four thousand years old."

That fellow must be a pressman! But anyway, imagine for a moment that you are an ant playing about in some farmer's field. Well, you see this great cloud coming from the distance and because you are a Wise Ant you scurry as fast as you can to the nearest tree and you shin up that tree with all six or eight, or whatever it is, legs. Then you get a first-class view of the world beneath you.

The farmer stops his chuffing tractor and gets down and opens the gate to the field, then he gets back on the tractor and chuffs away through the gateway and into the field. Then after he has scratched his head a bit, lit a cigarette, and done a mighty spit he hitches a plough up behind the tractor. And then what was your world, the smooth surface of your world with nice green grass and good clumps of weeds, gets in a state of turmoil. The farmer is ploughing. He goes on ploughing and ploughing, and he is deep ploughing, too, so all the surface of your world, which is that field, is broken up and the inner soil comes to the surface and everything is thoroughly messed up. Your friends in the ant colony disappear for ever. One of the plough blades saw to that in very decisive fashion. The ant colony was tipped upside down, and then great clods of earth rained down on them and after that one of those blade things at the end of the plough sliced right through the earth covering the deceased colony, and all the sides caved in even more. On the next pass down the field one of the rear wheels of the tractor pressed everything down deep.

Well, you, the last ant in all the world—your world is

the field, remember—shudder with fright. Everything has taken on a new look. There are great cliffs of earth standing up where before there was smooth earth and perhaps grass. There is nothing that you know left any more. But if you were given long life—I don't know how long an ant lives—you would see the winds and the rains beat down the ploughed up soil until everything became smooth again. But before that, perhaps, the farmer or his boy would come along with a seeder which is another device which turns up the earth a bit and scatters seed all over the place, and that seeder would be followed by hordes of birds. So you, poor ant, had better keep your tail down tight or you will lose it.

But that is how things go on on this Earth. There is what we of the Earth call a mighty civilization, New York, for instance; (is it mighty after Watergate?) supposing the end of a cycle had come, there would be terrific earthquakes, bigger earthquakes than you had ever dreamed possible, and you wouldn't dream about them either because you wouldn't live through them. The earthquakes would open chasms in the earth and buildings would fall in, chasms would extend perhaps half a mile deep into the earth, and all the buildings which were New York would fall in. Then the earth would close again, and there would be a few wriggles, and in course of time there would be no trace whatever of that mighty civilization.

The waters would change their course. The Hudson would disappear into the earth, the seas would sweep over part of the Earth perhaps, and perhaps New York's site would become the seabed, and everything that you knew of New York would have disappeared.

It's not true, though, to say that everything is lost without trace for ever and ever amen, because there have

161

been most interesting reports from deep-miners. They have been digging for coal, perhaps, and far down in the depths of their mine they have come across (and this is true) a figure buried in coal, a figure which might be fifteen feet long. They may also come across certain artefacts, and there have been such artefacts found and placed in Museums; there have been cycles and cycles on this Earth. If you go to a farm and look out across the farm land you can't say what sort of crop there was ten years ago, can you? You can't say what sort of crop there was twenty years ago, not even five years ago, not even one year ago, because everything has been ploughed down. Perhaps the farmer has had a very good crop which has depleted the earth, so he ploughs the land and lets it lie fallow for a year. After that he ploughs it again and plants a different crop, and so it goes on. The earth, too, is ploughed by earthquakes, and after the earthquakes come the floods and the tornadoes which blow the topsoil and smooth everything off and make sure that there is no trace of that which went before.

So, young man, you who write and tell me that I am not telling the truth, you are talking through the back of your neck. You don't know the first thing about all this, so the sooner you read all my books, and believe them, then the better for you.

Mrs. Mary MacMaggot of the Maggotorium, Toadsville, is a great herb fan. She firmly believes that people who take chemicals, and that means chemical drugs and all that sort of stuff, should have their brains tested; Mrs. Mary MacMaggot is absolutely convinced that you get good only from herbs. She thinks the rest of the pills, potions, liniments and lotions are just a device to make money for the drug houses.

Actually, there isn't any difference usually between the

drugs we get out of herbs and the drugs which are made in a factory. You know how it all happens, don't you? Well, let's take as our example a herb which is rich in iron. Now, the iron in that plant does not grow there provided by a benevolent Nature who knows that in time Mrs. MacMaggot will want an iron tonic. The iron came from the ground, and I am going to advise you to look on things something like this; all plants are cellulose, they are like cellulose sponges, and the cells in the sponges are filled with the life material of the plant; the cellulose is a form of skeleton, a form of support for the plant. So this particular plant that we are examining is very partial to soil which has a strong iron-ore element in it. It grows well in such circumstances, and the iron-ore is absorbed by the far-spreading roots of the plant and is then taken up by the sap and conveyed through all the cellulose tissues of the plant. There it is lodged in those cavities just as one can mop up dirty water with a sponge and get the sediment lodged in the cells of the sponge. Well, along comes a herbalist, grabs a handful of iron-bearing plants and messes about with them—perhaps he makes a tea of them, perhaps he mashes them up, but anyway he makes some awful unsavoury goo and takes the stuff. If he was lucky and he's got hold of a plant which had been successful in getting a good quantity of iron-ore he feels better for it. But if he finds a barren sort of plant then he says some naughty words and goes on to some pills.

All the big drug houses send research teams into exotic parts of the world, such as to the interior of Brasil. There the research people find all manner of plants which grow nowhere else in the world perhaps, because Brasil is truly a wonderful, wonderful country for its natural resources.

The plants are carefully noted, photographed, checked, and then bundled up and sent to research laboratories

163

where they are again examined in the light of information which has been obtained from natives, perhaps a native witch doctor uses this herb or that herb for curing barrenness or rheumatism, or something else. Well, the native witch doctors are usually right, they have generation after generation of passed-on experience to guide them, so you can be sure that if they say that such-and-such a plant is good for this or that complaint they are perfectly correct.

The research teams break down the plants, analyse them, make them into essences, make them into crystals, and they find out every single item about the plant, what it consists of, what it has secreted, and all the rest. And as is very frequently the case they can isolate a certain chemical which is responsible for the cures claimed by the witch doctors. Then, having that chemical further analysed, they can copy it exactly. So we have the chemical of the plant merely duplicated by the chemical in the laboratory, the manmade thing, and the manmade thing has a great advantage over the herbal chemical because there is no method of telling the potency of the herbal chemical, there might indeed be none. But if a thing is copied and manufactured in the laboratory then one can at all times prescribe an absolutely accurate dose.

I am thinking particularly of curare. Certain of the Amazon Brazilians—they call them Indians—used curare extract on arrows or spears, and if they shoot an arrow so coated at an animal the animal keels over, paralysed. But there is a lot of hit or miss because, again, in a herb which grows in the ground you can't be sure of your dosage. Years ago it was found that curare was useful to surgeons in paralysing a patient on the operating table and making his muscles relax. But when the herb was administered the results were uncertain, either the poor wretch was killed, or, often, he did not get a strong enough dose to be effective. But now that the drug curare is manufactured artificially there is no risk because at all times there is an exact dosage. So, Mrs. Mary Mac-Maggot, it's a good thing that we can have factory made chemical drugs which permit us to prescribe and dose with accuracy. Just think if you had to go out and chew up a pound of fennel before you found your cough was curing. Now you can take a little liquid and find that you can get your cough better really fast.

Another person writes and ask what I think of Arabs and Jews. Well, to tell you the truth, I don't think anything particular about them because while on Earth they are much the same type of people. Arabs and Jews were very friendly indeed just a few years ago, they mingled, Arabs in Jewish communities and Jews in Arab communities, and they were on the closest terms possible, there was no dispute between them, no dispute at all. But, you know, one of the facts of life is that love and hate are very similar, very close, you can have absolute love for a person which turns to absolute hatred almost overnight. Or you can have a most vicious bitter enemy, and then you can find that you love her almost before you know what is happening. It is because the chemicals are wrong in the two people concerned. It might be that Arabs and Jews have changed their eating habits somewhat, and so that the chemical intake leads to the opposition of their vibrations. If a person's vibrations are not compatible with another person's then we have hatred, and the vibrations are very often governed by the sort of food we eat because the food gives us our chemical intake, that is why in so many cases mega-vitamin treatment works wonders, and in other cases it can have no effect at all. So if we got a bunch of Jews and a bunch of Arabs and we fed them on the same stuff perhaps they would get on together and not try to cut each other's throat behind their back, so to speak. But I know, or knew, quite a lot of good Arabs, and I now know quite a lot of good Jews. Unfortunately I have met one or two bad ones as well, but then I have also met some bad Buddhists!

Often I get letters from Germany really giving me a working over because my books are not published in German. I can't help that. There was quite a campaign against me in Germany started up by a few fellows who were jealous because I wrote about Tibet, jealous because I wrote true books about Tibet, and so quite a press campaign was started against me. But it seems to me that the Germans are an unlovely people, it seems to me that they are the trouble-makers of Europe, they are so humourless, so deadpan, so righteous. So much so that I have had to decide that I wouldn't have my books published in Germany. I cannot stand these literal people, and I have often written to people in Germany and given them my honest opinion which is that it would have been better for the rest of Europe, perhaps, if the Russians had taken over the whole of Germany. If you look at history you will find that the Germans have made an awful commotion in the world, all the way back to the time of Attila the Hun.

So Mr. German, who is being so cross because he can't get my books in German, I don't want them published in German, and I wouldn't care two hoots—I couldn't care even half a hoot—what Germans think about it.

A gent here, I am sure he is a gent by the way he writes, believes that it must be wonderful to be an author. You don't do any work, you just walk about a room dictating to a staff of secretaries who hang on every word that the author utters and then struggle to put those words into beautiful prose that will hypnotize a publisher into paying wonderful royalties.

This fellow thinks that all authors are millionaires, all authors fly about the world with first-class tickets, or perhaps I should say first-class credit cards, and drive whacking great sports cars or Rolls Royces. Do you think I could take a minute or two to tell him to wake up? It's not so easy as all that. I believe the late Edgar Wallace had a formula which was like a skeleton of a book, and he kept on ringing the changes, having about six or seven different sets of plots whereby he hung different names, different locations, and different crimes on to that book skeleton, and then he used to stride about the room with a long cigarette holder in his hand dictating out of the corner of his mouth (you have to if you are smoking at the same time) to two or three typists. Well, that is mass production. The average poor wretch of an author doesn't do it that way. Anyway, do you know what true books need? Let me tell you.

First of all, if you are going to write a true book you must have had some true experiences, you must have had some horrible experiences which scar you for life. People who have been in prison camps, for instance, are never the same, they are scarred, often their health has deteriorated and is deteriorating as a result of their experiences. So they have the knowledge of certain things. But then they have to be able to write, they have to be able to put words describing their experiences in passable interesting form. If they can do that then they have to be sure that their experiences are such that people want to read about them.

After they have typed the book they have to get a publisher to read the typescript, but first of all before a publisher will consider such a typescript, you have to

167

have certain mechanical disciplines. You seem to be interested, so I will tell you about it.

You have to type on one side of the page without too many mistakes. You have to have double-line spacing. You count ten words to each line, and twenty-five lines to each page. That gives you two hundred and fifty words to a page. Now a chapter in my average book consists of twenty pages, that means five thousand words, and I usually have twelve chapters which adds up to sixty thousand words. And when you've got up to sixty thousand words you find you have left out something important so you add on a few words more.

It is, it seems, very necessary that you get your chapters much about the same length because you don't get one man to set up your book, the book is divided between a number of type-setters, and if one gets short chapters and another gets long chapters—well, there might be trouble with the Union or something. So it's better to get your chapters fairly even, about five thousand words to a chapter, perhaps with a bit shorter chapter in the beginning and a bit shorter chapter at the end. So if you can do that and your typing is neat enough, then you may get a publisher to read it, and reading a typescript is the first step to getting it published.

By far the best method of getting a book to your publisher is to use the services of an agent. I have a very good one indeed. Throughout the years we are not just agent and client, but I consider Mr. Knight as my friend. He is that jewel of agents, a completely honest man. It is, obviously, absolutely necessary that your agent be honest and work on your behalf. The name of the firm is Stephen Aske, of 39 Victoria Street, London, England.

But I must warn you that if you send muck which will never have a chance of getting printed, then an agent is justified in charging you a reading fee. So if you, full of literary zeal, feel a compelling urge to write then you would be well advised to get in touch with an agent such as Mr. Knight enclosing return postage, and you will ask him his advice—is there a market for such-and-such a thing, etc. If there is he will tell you so, and he will undoubtedly suggest that you do a synopsis of perhaps five thousand words telling briefly what the book is going to be about.

Don't send stuff without writing first, and don't expect an agent—or an author either—to answer your letter unless you put in entirely adequate postage. An agent has to pay for printing, he has to pay for typing, he has to pay for time, overheads such as electricity and heating, etc., taxes on his building, rent on his building, and if you do not observe the decencies of life and enclose adequate postage your prospective agent may just do what I should do—toss the stuff in the garbage.

A good agent is invaluable. He will get in touch with publishers in other countries, and he will get after publishers to pay on time, and believe me, some publishers do not!

But if you think that you are going to make a fortune out of writing—go out and pick up a shovel and become a builder or something like that. These are the people who make money nowadays, the author, unless he's got something particular to say, often does not make enough to live on, and a hungry author is a horrible sight indeed.

People write to me asking what I recommend in music, people who want to be elevated—raised up, given spiritual uplift and all that. Well, it is very appropriate at this moment because I have just had a letter from a young man in England who takes me to task because of what I have said about present day "music." Not only that, but he sends me a sample of what he considers to be good music. I have no record player so a friend of mine tried it, and apparently the result is that the poor friend is almost a friend no longer because the music was "jangle, jangle, bang, bang" like a procession of mad garbage collectors with St. Vitus Dance beating garbage can lids together. Hey—I wish you wouldn't send me some of these hard rock records. My! You'll make me lose my few friends if you do. So take warning from this; I have no record player.

I believe that music should be soothing, it should be the type of thing which makes a feeling of goodness, the sort of music which raises your vibrations.

I believe that a lot of the neurotic tendencies in life nowadays are caused by unsuitable "music" because, you see, when you listen to music your own personal vibrations vibrate in sympathy or as a harmonic to that which you are hearing. So if you are listening to a lot of disturbing jive (I think that's what the stuff is called) your own personal vibrations will be set on edge. It seems to me that so many nervous complaints have been caused by imitation stereo belching out hard rock at enormous volume and really upsetting one's psyche. So if you want to progress spiritually you will start listening to some of the old masters, some of the definite classicals, some of the music which the younger generation will not listen to and perhaps never have listened to because they think everything to do with "the establishment" is against their interests.

We get much the same type of thing with the radio nowadays; one is trying to listen to a good musical programme and, over here on the North American continent at least, we get interrupted with hysterical announcements that Bloggs Pills will cure everything from constipation

170

to corns. Well, that is very bad—not the constipation or corns—but the sudden frenetic announcement uttered in hysterical tones because it completely shatters the soothing vibrations which had built up through good music. So if you want to listen to good music, get it on records or on tape so that you don't have a hysterical young man bawling the love song of patent medicine.

"Dr. Rampa," the letter said, "you have done fourteen books so far, are you going to go on writing? I think you should go on writing—I think you should write until the end."

Well, madam, you refer to fourteen books. This is the fifteenth, this "Twilight," and why shouldn't I write some more, as you say? After all, I might get as far as Midnight. Who knows? It depends on the public demand because a publisher won't publish books unless there is a demand for them, and there is no guarantee, you know, that an author can write a book and be sure of its acceptance. An author is like a blind man, he has to feel his way. So if you want more books why not write to my publisher and ask for them? If you want better covers—and I surely hope you do!—then why not write to my publisher and tell him so? And if you do not like the fading yellow paper which the publisher uses, well, please tell him; do not tell me because I assure you on all the holy books there are that I have no say in the matter of covers, illustrations, the type of paper used or the size of print. So you beat up the publisher instead, it's something I cannot do.

People write to Miss Ku'ei and to Mrs. Fifi Greywhiskers. Of course these two ladies are no longer on this Earth, a cat's life is a very short life, you know. They live about seven times faster than a human, so a year in our

171

time is equal to seven years in a cat's time. Now Miss Cleopatra is, in cat time, nearly sixty years of age!

Miss Cleopatra Rampa is a seal-pointed Siamese cat, and I say in all seriousness that she is the most intelligent person I have ever met, no matter whether that person be human or what. Miss Cleopatra is by far the most intelligent, most sympathetic, and most loving of all. She looks after me.

As you know, or should know by now, I am ill, and a short time ago I was very ill indeed and it was enjoined upon me that I should not move more than I really had to. Well, Miss Cleopatra took it upon herself to sit by me at night; she sat on a little bedside table which I have, actually a hospital bed-table, and she would sit upright all night, and if I dared move more than she thought necessary she would reach out and give me a thoroughly hard slap as if I was a bad child whom she was disciplining!

She does do rounds just like a hospital nurse. When she is not "on duty" full time by my bedside she will come in several times during the night and very quietly jump on my bed (of course I am not supposed to know!) and then she will creep stealthily up beside me and peer intently into my face to make sure I am breathing satisfactorily. If I am she will quietly go away. If I am not she makes a commotion which fetches other people.

All the time I have known her I have never known Cleopatra to be irritable or cross or anything except absolutely sweet tempered and reasonable, and if there is a thing that one doesn't like her to do one can just tell her so in an ordinary normal voice and she will not do it any more. Buttercup, for example, did not like Little People sitting on her hats which presumably, from a woman's point of view, is reasonable. She told Cleo without anger, without irritation, and Cleo hasn't done it since.

Fat Taddy lives with us as well. She is a blue-point Siamese cat, much heavier than Cleo, and she is not so intelligent in a material, physical sort of way, although compared to other cats she is highly intelligent. Her particular talent lies in the realms of telepathy. She is the most telepathic creature I have ever met, and when she wants to she can get over her message as loudly as a public address system blaring in one's ears. She is the responsibility of Cleo who more or less shepherds her around and sees that she behaves herself. But Cleo is my special guardian. Taddy is more interested in guarding the food!

People write to me, as you may have gathered, and ask all sorts of strange questions, they ask all sorts of personal questions too. For instance, they want to know my age which is nothing to do with anyone else. Some of them want to know if I get the old age pension, and I am able to tell them that I am not able to get the old age pension for what I consider to be a strange reason; I spent some time in South America and because I have not been back in Canada for ten years I cannot get the old age pension. So any of you who are "senior citizens" might be interested to know that according to Canadian law one has to be in the country for a complete and entire ten years—even if one is a naturalized Canadian citizen—before one can get the old age pension. In 1975 I shall have been back in Canada for ten years, so then if I am still alive I have to sign a form so that another person can collect the old age pension for me as I cannot go in person to do it.

I am also asked if Mrs. Rampa still lives with me, and I was about to say, "Well, obviously she does," but in these

173

days of sudden or instantaneous divorces it's not so obvious any more is it? So let me say—yes, Mrs. Rampa does live with me, and so does Buttercup, Mrs. S. M. Rouse, who lives with us as a member of our family and as a very important member of our family at that.

Sometimes I get offensive letters from Australia. I had one letter from Australia from a man by the name of Samuels. He wrote to me in a thoroughly unpleasant manner saying that there had been no word from Mrs. Rampa and if I was genuine why didn't Mrs. Rampa say so. Well, actually, she has done so, many, many times. But I'll tell you what; I'll let Mrs. Rampa start the next chapter with a few uninhibited words unguided by me, undirected by me, so she can say what she likes. So, Mr. Publisher, will you put on some soft music, dim the lights over our Readers, and prepare to illuminate the spotlight, because for the next chapter we will have Mrs. Rampa start it.

CHAPTER ELEVEN

Let me here introduce Mrs. S. A. Rampa. I have offered her the opportunity of saying what she wants to say, so here it is:—

"It had been suggested that I should make a small contribution toward this, the fifteenth book, write a chapter, for instance, and at first the thought gave me quite a shock.

"No! I would not presume to try for a chapter. But as

the Author agrees, I will be very happy to make a few comments.

"This evening I finished reading the typescript of Chapter Nine which was hot off the typewriter, and I believe Chapter Ten is also completed, but that one I have not yet read. So if I do not hurry I will be too late for this book.

"As I was going about my evening duties such as watering the plants, preparing our supper, and attending to the very small needs of Cleopatra and Tadalinka, my thoughts were dwelling on the material I had been reading in the pages of 'Twilight.'

"First of all I would like to mention that when Lobsang Rampa refers to 'my Wife' or 'Mrs. Rampa' it is still the same creature who is known by other names in previous books, it is still 'Ma' of 'Living with the Lama,' or 'Mrs. Old Man' of 'Beyond the Tenth', and 'Ra'ab' of 'Candlelight.' It seems appropriate that you should be assured that Lobsang Rampa is a loyal and devoted person, and is not in the habit of frequently changing his partner, and I hope the same can be said of myself.

"Many things have been said for and against us just the same as they have criticized the President of the United States of America who has just reluctantly relinquished his position as President.

"Like President Nixon we have suffered greatly at the hands of the press, and during the past few days we have been reminded that the critics with the least knowledge have the most to say. Were it not so these people would be engaged in formulating better conditions instead of trying to break down the best efforts of a few others who are striving to do some good for their fellow men.

"But criticism is not my purpose tonight, rather do I

175

desire to make a few comments about the Author of this book, 'Twilight.'

"Dr. Rampa is not the gruff, embittered old man portrayed by some thoughtless persons. Indeed he is extremely sick and therefore has enough cause for gruffness and irritability, but he is not horrid and touchy. Instead, he is continually thinking of others, and during the past week I have noticed more closely than ever how great is his compassion toward those who are in distress. Last night we listened together, as did people around the world, to the tragic announcement of the impending end of a Presidency, and Dr. Rampa was so deeply moved by the sadness of it all that he spent a more than usually sleepless night. One of the things which causes this extreme sadness was the attitude of the reporters, they did not merely do the job of reporting but, to repeat expressions used by another listener, they were SPRAYED WITH HATE.

"Perhaps I should apologize for the length of my commentary, for it had been intended that this would be just a few lines. There is just one further point, and I want to put it on record now, for it may be the only opportunity I will have, that I personally owe my outlook and my whole attitude to life to this man who has sacrificed so much to help us, and especially to help me.

"Although life is not always easy, one does not mind so much if one can see where one is going, and, as we have been told often enough, there is no short cut to tranquility. From personal experience I can state definitely that however difficult, however impossible we consider ourselves to be, with a little effort and REGULAR practice we can overcome many of our problems, making it easier to live with others, and, just as important, easier to live with ourselves. In my own case, the Teachings and, even

176

more important, the EXAMPLE of Lobsang Rampa has been the greater factor in assisting me to come to terms with myself, resulting I hope in my being a somewhat better person.

"I do not know whether there will be space left in the book for this modest contribution because it had all been planned before I could arrange my thoughts. However, the writing has been enjoyable, and I wish there had been more space so I could tell of various incidents depicting the very compassionate side of the nature, the side which is not familiar to everyone, not always recognized, but which nevertheless is a very real part of the Lobsang Rampa make-up. Still, there may be another opportunity. Who knows? But I know this; in answer to that offensive man in Australia who wrote demanding that I prove something let me say that—yes, I know without possibility of error that Lobsang Rampa is who he claims to be and that all his books are true."

Well, I had hoped that if we were going to have illustrations they could have borne the signature of S. M. Rouse, and I also hoped that if blocks were made for illustrations, the foregoing paragraphs by Mrs. Rampa could have borne her signature because there is always some creep ready to say, "Oh by golly, he wrote it himself." (But he didn't!)

As for this proof business, well there is no point in trying to prove a thing to anyone because if a person wants to believe then he will believe, and if a person doesn't want to believe then no amount of proof—no amount of proof at all—will convince him. So—you make your own choice.

But another thing I have been asked is about books, what books should people read. Well, I can't give a whole list of books because I don't have many myself, but two books in particular have greatly impressed me, and I will give you the two titles and the necessary data. The first is "The Spaceships of Ezekiel" by Josef F. Blumrich. That is a Corgi Book, and I can most truly recommend it. The Author nearly laughed his head off when his son told him about U.F.O.'s, and the Author is a NASA scientist, a man well qualified to know about U.F.O.'s and all that. He was so amused by his son's stupid belief in such things that he set out to prove that there couldn't be any "flying saucers."

The more he tried to prove the more convinced he became that there were such things, and in the end as a designer he was able to design the type of space ship which was written about in the times of Ezekiel, but it is a thoroughly good book and one that I absolutely recommend, so put on your running shoes and rush around to your local book store and buy it, and you will see that I am a good book critic!

Another extraordinarily good book is called "Timeless Earth." It is written by Peter Kolosimo. I believe it was first written in French, but it has been translated into English by Paul Stevenson, and it is published by University Books Inc. (I am glad they have some "inc" because they need it for printing books, don't they?) This is another book which really will hold your interest. It tells the truth, and it should be in the Library of every serious thinking person. While you are rushing around for the space ships book, how about picking up "Timeless Earth" as well? You might find your education has been improved thereby.

Hey! I'm being good in this book, aren't I? I'm not just answering your questions, I am also recommending other authors! But let us get on with some more of our questions and answers.

Let me make a confession here; my sight is very poor so I have been "cheating" by picking out the letters which are typed because sometimes people write to me and their handwriting reminds me of the squiggles which would be made by a spider suffering from St. Vitus Dance who had just crawled out of the inkwell. No doubt many, many questions which would be most interesting have been overlooked because I COULD NOT READ THE WRITING!

There is a question here, though, which doesn't at all follow in the writer's supposition. This young man says, "You say that we are all immortal, however wouldn't it be logical to say that if we have no end we would also have no beginning? Wouldn't it make it more logical to make it go both ways?"

No, I don't think so, I don't see that at all. After all, a thing has to begin otherwise it is not, and once it has begun why shouldn't it keep on? In theory, you see, if a person could exactly replace all his body cells in precisely the same pattern as the ones he was replacing then he would go on for ever and ever, wouldn't he? A person wears out for the simple reason that the mechanism which replaces cells increasingly has a defective memory, and so the cells which are replaced and the cells which are replacing are somewhat different and grow increasingly different.

I, quite bluntly, cannot see any reason why a thing should not start but not end, and, anyway, Mr. L., what do YOU mean by "no ending"? We go on and on, there is an end to the human body, the physical body, and then we go on into the astral, and in the fullness of time there is an end to the astral body. In other words, we die quite painlessly in the astral and pass on to another dimension, and so on, and so on, ad infinitum.

"Is there such a thing as a half or quarter dimensional world? This question has been puzzling me for a long time."

No, there is no such thing. You have to have a complete dimension otherwise you would get interaction. You get a similar state of things on a very very minor scale when this world and our negative world come in too close proximity. You get people disappearing, such as at the Bermuda Triangle, but these cannot be called half or quarter dimensions, it is just a misfortunate (not unfortunate!) happening.

"Dr. Rampa, why do the press find such sick joy in persecuting you just because you come along with a very special task that needed to be dealt with? Do they not believe that you are perfectly truthful in everything you say and do? You have rights, you know, and they should respect them."

Of course I have done nothing to make the press like me. But I have done nothing to make the press dislike me, either. You see, press people come along with a fierce, threatening demand, they demand that one give them an interview and say whatever they—the interviewers—want said, and if the victim doesn't agree then he is set up for press persecution.

Some years ago I received an offer from a T.V. station. They wanted me to go on television and tell the truth of "The Rampa Story." I was perfectly willing to do so because all that I have written and said is the truth. I am whom I claim to be and I can do all that I write about. So—there I was, all ready to go on television. But then to my profound amazement, I found that they did not want TRUTH, instead they wanted me to read a prepared statement saying that I was a fake. Well, I wasn't a fake so I would not read the statement, so I was not permitted to go on television and tell the simple truth. Instead I was persecuted by the press.

I wrote to the Press Council in England complaining of all the vicious lies which were being written about me, but the Press Council thought the press should have freedom to write whatever they wanted to write. I also wrote to the Governors of the T.V. station and they thought that a television producer should be given the freedom to say whatever he wanted to say on television and to require that other people do the same. So it seems to me that the press, the radio, and the television are a closed shop. Now, I am going to ask you a question; if you were attacked by the press or on the radio or on television, and you knew quite definitely that what they were writing or saying about you was lies, how could you refute those lies? Remember, you can't get published in the press unless they want to publish what you write, and you can't broadcast or appear before the television cameras unless someone wants you to. So there is no way in which you can defend yourself. Someone may say, "Well, take legal action." Yes, fine, but that takes a lot of money, and it cannot be done unless you have a lot of money. I tried to do that against a man in the U.S.A., a man who was pretending that he was publishing my books, or rather publishing books written by me, when they weren't by me at all. He was making use of my name, but I tried to get a lawyer to act for me and because I lacked the money to pay the fantastic advance he expected nothing was done. I have had to see people use my name, misuse my name, pretend to be me, and all the rest of it, and there is nothing I can do. If I had the money, or if some lawyer would be paid by results, then, by golly, I certainly would make a case against a few people, against a young punk, for instance, who pretends he is my bosom friend and that he is selling articles direct from "Lobsang Rampa's workshop." As I told you before, I do not have a workshop, I do not make articles any more, and if people pretend they are my friend and that they can use my name, then remember there are only two people who are making things designed by me—Mr. Sowter in England, and Mr. Orlowski in Prince Edward Island, Canada.

"You talk about a World Leader whose body is presently being prepared on the Earth and for the Great Entity to come and animate it; do you know where the body is presently living? Could the entity who is going to come and take over the body be the reincarnation of Jesus, Mohammed, or Gautama?"

Oh yes, I know precisely where the body is, and I have actually seen the body. But, of course, I wouldn't say where he is or we would find some crummy pressman rushing off and coming back with some fantastic entirely imaginary article. I definitely know where the body is.

No, Jesus, Mohammed or Gautama are not reincarnations and they are not coming to take over this particular body. You see, there is a special group of Entities who come down to Earth at certain times. I really hesitate to use a term such as "White Brotherhood" because there are so many stupid people who think they will start up a cult called the White Brotherhood, or the Dark Donkeys or something else. There are so many sick people nowadays that they seize on anything which they feel might sound plausible. But there is a definite group of Entities . . . and you cannot take a correspondence course with them and you will not find them associated with any of these crazy cultists on this Earth . . . who come down to this world, and of course also go to other worlds, to set an example as Teachers. It would be such a waste of time if they had to get born here when all they have to do would take, perhaps, a year. So they take over a specially prepared body, and when their task is done the body disappears in some way which we need not discuss here.

"You always talk about humans and animals. Are we not animals too?"

Yes, of course we are, not very nice animals either, some of us. But I am merely following what one might term a pattern in referring to humans and animals. It makes it clear that I am referring to one species—human—or another species—say cat. And, as I have been telling you previously, Miss Cleopatra is the most intelligent person I know no matter whether we are going to consider animal or human.

Hey! What's the matter with you? Your question is, "Please tell us how to use a crystal. I would like to see the answer to that one in your next book. Should we make the room pitch dark before we experiment? Should we put the glass in a safe place so that it won't be used for other purposes? Should we use a little imagination in the matter of making something appear, or what?"

Well! I really thought I had made the matter very clear on how to use a crystal. Now supposing you do not have a crystal, supposing you use a glass of water instead; well, you get a new glass, an absolutely plain glass without any pattern on it, without any etching, without any scratches, in fact, a fairly expensive glass which has no flaws so far as you can see. Then you carefully wash it and when you have rinsed off all the soapsuds you fill it with water right up to the top so that you've got a menuscus (the menuscus is that bump which appears when you slightly over-fill a glass). The glass full of water is now set on a table or somewhere dark and you make sure that your room is dark or dim, obviously you must be able to see the glass, you must be able to see your hands in front of you, but you do not need to be able to see to read the newspaper. I give you that just as a guide. The correct amount of darkness is when colours begin to disappear.

Having the right conditions, you breathe deeply a few times and settle yourself so that you are comfortable, there must be no strain, no muscle which is twitching, no nerve which is flapping. And then you gaze in the direction of the glass of water but you do not gaze actually at it, you look through it with your eyes unfocused, imagine that you are focusing on infinity. Got that clear? You are looking in the direction of the glass and you are deliberately defocusing your eyes imagining that you are looking at some invisible spot in space. You just sit there letting your mind take over, and the first thing you will notice is cloudiness, the water seems to turn milky white, and then, provided you do not jerk or fall off your chair with shock, the milky whiteness dissipates and then you see pictures. And that is all there is to it. You do not have to imagine things, why should you when you can see the real things?

After you have used your glass you tip out the water, you rinse it and dry it, and then you wrap it up in a black cloth and you use it for nothing else at all.

If you are using a crystal then you do the same in the matter of gazing at it, but after you have used it you wrap it up in a black cloth because if bright sunlight falls upon it you will spoil its power in much the same way as if you allow sunlight to fall on a film which has been unrolled—the thing will be no good after.

"I would like to know what you think of gambling?"

Well, that's easy. I have said that several times in my books. I am completely opposed to gambling, and although quite frequently people will send me sweepstake tickets and all that sort of thing, I have never in my life won anything at all—not even a cent, so there!

"I cannot seem to find out where the zone for cats is in the astral world. How do you go about finding such zones?"

You have just been taking me to task in a previous question saying why do I refer to humans and animals, because aren't humans animals as well? So now you want to know the zone for animals, so let me say to you, aren't humans animals as well, and if humans can go to a zone why can't four-legged animals? The answer is—they can. Miss Ku'ei and Mrs. Fifi Greywhiskers are great friends of mine, they are in the astral plane waiting for me. I have another Girl Cat Friend there called Cindy, and Cindy comes down to this Earth in actual physical form to see me and to give me messages—that is perfectly true! So let me tell you that animals, if they are of sufficient spiritual status, can go to any plane of existence to which humans of the same status can go. In other worlds, you know, animals are not treated as inferior creatures, they are not "dumb animals" any longer on other worlds, and to a person who is telepathic, as I am, there is no such thing as a dumb animal. While we are talking about animals, does it ever occur to you that the only bad or vicious animals are those who have been made so by humans? Normally animals are born "good" and they stay so unless messed up by humans. So the answer to your question is this; animals do go to the same zones as humans, so when you pass over quite definitely you can be met by an animal you love AND WHO LOVES YOU!

The last few days here have been very very hot, unbearably hot, in fact. But now at this moment the temperature has dropped about thirty degrees and we are having a thunderstorm, and some poor souls are getting married, or probably they are already married. It is a strange custom here in Calgary that when a couple has just been married and are driving along away from the place of marriage they make as much commotion as they can. The bridal car and all the cars attached to that bridal retinue have horns sounding all the time, and the uproar is truly formidable. I can't see any sense in it personally because how is it going to help a marriage to have blaring horns disturbing everyone?

Another thing that puzzles me here in Calgary is the Fire Department, the Police and the Ambulances. They have the loudest sirens I have ever heard anywhere. Not only that, but the ambulance sirens wobble and warble and really could just about scare a nervous patient to death. Where I live there is a sort of conjunction of concrete buildings, and for some strange reason the sound echoes and re-echoes and echoes again, and quite truly seems to be increased in volume because of some architectural idiosyncrasy. Anyway, the noise goes on day and night, and here the traffic is unceasing. I have never seen the road outside without loads of cars. Throughout the whole of the twenty-four hours of the day and night there is a continuous flow of fast cars, and I often lie in my bed and look out of the window and wonder where all the people are going, unceasingly moving the whole time nonstop, day and night. There are too many cars here and too much noise. But I suppose some will write to me now and say I am jealous because I haven't a car or something. People do that, you know, people write and tell me I am bitter. I didn't know it, I don't feel that I am bitter. I have my own problems and I cope with them as best I can, so there it is.

When I was in the hospital last time I had a learner Christian Chaplain come and try to con me into a bit of

186

religion, and before I said anything except that I was a Buddhist he said, "Oh, and do you feel guilty about it, or bitter that you are not a Christian?" So what do you think about that?! I could have replied, "No, but you look a bit guilty about being a Christian."

It does seem so strange that so many doctors and so many parsons try to cough up a sort of pseudo-psychology; they try to analyze one's behaviour entirely on text book learning, and they forget that a Buddhist may have a different outlook on life than does a Christian. But let's get back to some of these questions and answers. But first of all let me read you something from a letter written to me by Mr. Borge Langeland. He says, "I am happy to learn that you are writing a fifteenth book. I don't know how to tell you how much your books have meant to us. If they weren't true I should lose all confidence in my ability to judge what to accept and what to reject. To you perhaps your aura work is the most important mission in this life, but I think that by writing your books and letting people in on some of the mysteries of life that some of us have been fumbling about trying to solve you have done far more good for humanity than by proving that there is an aura and that it can be photographed."

Well, Mr. Langeland, yes, you have my definite, definite assurance that all my books are absolutely true; these books are not fiction, they are truth. Not just truth as I see truth, but actuality truth.

Yes, the Great Thirteenth Dalai Lama did indeed bless me by placing both of his hands on my head IN A SPECIAL MANNER—that "in a special manner" is important because a very very gifted man as was the Great Thirteenth can pass on special powers, he can, in effect, speed up one's vibrations. This, by the way, is in answer to someone who wants to know about such things.

187

You probably know that years ago in England and, in fact, in many countries there was a quite definite belief that the King could cure illness, and if a King placed his hands on a sufferer then the sufferer would be cured. You get the same thing in the legend about Jesus where if a person could touch the robe which Jesus wore, then he or she would be cured of all illness. It is because such people have a different vibration, and when they see by their superior knowledge that another person has possibilities for improvement and a possibility for accepting an increase in vibration, they do that necessary gesture which does give the recipient an ineffable sense of well-being and power. And I am going to tell you that my abilities increased enormously from that act by the Dalai Lama.

You ask why one hand or why two hands. You tell me that people who go to Church and get blessed every Sunday don't seem to be any better or any worse because of it. Well, that is right enough. The Great Thirteenth used two hands in the same way that if you have an electric device you have to have two wires—two contacts—because just one would not "pass any current." As for your saying that people who go to Church are not improved by being touched with one hand or two hands—no, that is just what I have been telling you. You only get benefit if the person doing the touching is a superior person, not some poor parson or cleric who is just doing mumbo-jumbo because it's the easiest sort of job he knows, and anyway he doesn't know anything else. Oh no, as far as benefit comes from such a thing you could go out and ask anyone in the street to touch you on the head, you would be just as well off!

You ask what causes the Sun's rays to be reflected so brightly from the Moon. "We have sent men to the Moon and they have discovered that the Moon is not made of green cheese but of rocks and sand very similar to what is here on Earth. When the Sun's rays hit a high mountain top on Earth early in the morning or late at night the valley below remains in darkness. Since the rocks on the mountain top are similar to the rocks on the Moon why don't they reflect the rays down into the valley?"

Easy, my dear sir, easy; the surface of the Moon is very similar in its reflective power to that of gypsum, and gypsum, which is like plaster of paris, does indeed reflect. But in the case of the Moon the reflection is aided enormously because there is no air to absorb the light rays. Light rays, you know, consist of vibrations and if there is air then the vibrations are slowed by passage through that atmosphere. The Moon, as we know, has no atmosphere, thus the rays from the Sun reach the Moon unimpeded and are reflected unimpeded from the Moon's surface.

You ask about rocks on Earth, why do they not reflect the Sun's rays down into the valley. The answer to that is because the angle of incidence is different. You see, when you get rays of light coming down to mountain tops the rays are reflected upwards, or within a narrow arc, they are not reflected downwards, and you can easily try this out for yourself by having a fairly powerful light bulb suspended from the ceiling and that will represent the Sun. Then you sit on the floor with a hand mirror in your hand. You can then reflect the Sun's rays (actually the suspended lamp) back on to the ceiling or fairly high up on the walls around you, but without very acrobatic contortions you cannot reflect the rays down between your feet which will be considered as the valley. Is that clear?

The third question from this gentleman is a sensible

one, so let's answer it. He says, "You write that wars are necessary to control the population explosion and to give people an opportunity for self-sacrifice. What is the kharmic effect on such war heroes who perhaps give up their own life fighting for their country but in the process kill or maim many of their enemies that they have never even seen before? When, or if, they should meet again somewhere in the Hereafter would they ask, are you the S.O.B. who killed me? And how does someone gain merit for fighting a war and killing someone even if they lose their own life?"

The laws of kharma are different when a person is fighting in defence of his home, his family and his country, so that if you are ordered into the forces you really have no choice, you have to go. And once you are in the forces you come under a blanket protection so that the people who give the orders—basically the Governments —have to accept the kharmic results of those orders.

You, Private A.B., are sent to the war front. You have a rifle in your hands, and at a certain time you may be told to fire that rifle. You have to obey your orders or you may get killed for disobedience. So you pull the trigger and a bullet kills one of the enemy. The kharmic effect of that is not yours, you do not have to worry about it. The kharmic effect is assumed by the person or persons WHO ACTUALLY CAUSED THE WAR!

When you get to the "Other Side" you do not have to meet the person you killed or the person who killed you. Only if you have no dislike and no hatred of those persons can you meet them. Certainly you can gain merit by preventing atrocities. Suppose a little troop of men are able to ambush members of the opposition—the enemy— who were setting out to massacre a lot of women and children, perhaps they were going to set fire to the houses

190

after they had locked the inhabitants inside. Well, you and your small troop could kill perhaps twenty members of the assassination gang, but in doing so you would have saved possibly two thousand women, children, and old people, so the balance would be to the good, wouldn't it, and under that heading you would have "gained merit."

Mrs. Nancy Justice is an old friend of mine, we have been corresponding for—oh, I forget how long, but it's quite a long time. Now she writes in and she has some questions. So I think we ought to attend to Mrs. Nancy Justice, don't you? She says, "I am slightly clairvoyant. In your book 'Wisdom of the Ancients' you define clairvoyance as seeing through walls and beyond. What I mean is knowing what is going to happen before it happens, but I can do this to a limited degree only. I have an urge to crystal gaze or something of that sort. I know mirrors seem to draw my eyes, and I read somewhere of mirrors that were used once upon a time where they painted one side or something. Could you tell me how to do this?"

Well, Mrs. Justice, I have just been writing about crystals and how to use them, so I think that actually does answer most of your question, but very definitely I would not advise you to use a Black Mirror because if used carelessly they are very very dangerous things indeed and enable mischievous entities to work harm through you. So take my advice and have nothing whatever to do with these Black Mirrors. A crystal cannot harm you in any way at all.

You go on, "I see that you talk a lot about the astral and travelling by astral. Also I believe you when you say that no harm can come to you, but I am one of those strange persons who is deathly afraid of hypnotism, even self-hypnosis. What I wanted to ask you is, is it true that when you are deeply engrossed in reading something like reading a book to the point that you are not aware of outside influence, well, that is a form of hypnosis?"

No harm can happen when you are doing astral travel unless you are afraid. But then you can be harmed if you take fright even if you are crossing the road. You might run the wrong way.

I am definitely opposed to hypnosis. I am also opposed to self-hypnosis because it is so easy to do it the wrong way, easier to do it the wrong way than it is to do it the right way, in fact. So stay clear of all forms of hypnosis, they are bad. But rest quite assured that when you are reading a book you are not hypnotized. Instead you are merely interested and that is absolutely safe.

You give a third question, Mrs. Justice, and it is so applicable that I am going to answer it here now: You write, "You keep saying that to try all the different things in your book that nothing will ever happen to you like being possessed. Fine, but how did those people who are possessed get that way? What did they do or not do?"

That's a fair enough question. But you will remember just above that I have been telling you not to do hypnosis. I have been telling you not to use Black Mirrors. So if you do and try these things then you can easily get possessed. I am telling you throughout all my books how NOT to get possessed, and if you follow what I write then you cannot get possessed. But if you disregard what I am saying then you will get possessed, which is what you want to know about.

Black Mirrors, Black Magic, hypnosis and some of those ouija boards can lead you astray, you can get hypnotized with them, you can get possessed. And this is why I say time after time DON'T DO IT!

CHAPTER TWELVE

Everyone here is very busy; normally I like to type a lot of my books myself and then have Buttercup retype them on her Olympia typewriter. Hy Mendelson gave me a typewriter which I have named "the Yellow Peril" but I have not been able to use it much on this book, my health has not permitted, and so most of this book has been dictated on a Sony tape recorder—just a small pocket thing, so I can claim kinship with Mr. Nixon. He used Sony recorders for his Watergate tapes, I believe!

Buttercup is a marvellous typist; extremely fast and extraordinarily accurate. It is a matter of much jubilation when she makes a mistake because it's nice to tell her that she is not perfect after all. But we here at Rampa Residence owe a very great deal to Buttercup and without her we should have a much harder time. So—thank you, Buttercup Rouse.

Mrs. Rampa is a hard worker, too. She goes through the pages of the typescript with an eagle eye, and between them—Buttercup and Mrs. Rampa—not many mistakes get by, and if I make a mistake in my dictation . . . ! My goodness me, I never hear the last of it. Buttercup comes on me like ten tons of bricks, and there is no peace until I have rectified the error of omission or commission or some other mission. My sympathy, though, goes to the poor wretched typesetters who have to set up books, because it must be a horrifying thing indeed to have to set up in print a book which you find boring or in which you just can't get any interest. I would just hate to be a typesetter.

As I am sitting here in my wheelchair I can see our little river outside, and there are two boat loads of crazy people paddling away as if they were Red Indians on the warpath. The weather is quite cold, and our river is dangerous. It has silted up quite a lot and there are—for the size of the river—immense sandbanks which channel the water through a narrow space and so increase its speed and set up whirlpools. We are always reading that someone has been drowned or fished out of the water, and yet people still go in it on old tyres or anything they can dig up. Oh well, good for the Funeral Homes, I suppose!

Now, I've got another question here which I have already answered but I am going to answer it again in, possibly, a different form in order that someone may get a different slant on the thing. The question is: "What is meant by the statement: When the student is ready the Master appears?"

Too many people think that they know all and plenty more besides, they think that they just have to whistle and hordes of Masters come panting with eagerness to teach such a bright person. It doesn't happen that way at all.

You know those kettles, you shove them on the gas or electricity, and when the water boils they let out a horrendous hoot? Well, people are like that. When their vibrations reach a certain pitch, that is, when they are "ready", a Master somewhere, either on the Earth or in the astral, can pick up a vibration which says, metaphorically of course, "Hey boss, I'm ready, come and teach me all you know!" So after the Master has given a luxurious stretch and a hearty scratch, he might get to his feet, or even to his astral feet, and come along to give a hand.

But nearly always the person who thinks that he or she is such a brilliant student that he or she is ready—well, they are the ones who just are not ready, and no matter how much they hoot or let off steam, until their vibrations reach the right pitch or frequency—no Master will appear. So if a Master doesn't appear it is proof positive that you are not ready.

Who is this? Ester A. Moray. Okay Ester Moray, here is your second question: "How does race kharma affect an individual?"

Before a person reincarnates to Earth that person goes to what we may somewhat humorously regard as a travel agent in the astral. Actually it is a Council of Advisors. But the person who is going to come back to Earth knows what has to be done, where he or she has to go, and what the circumstances should be for doing that particular task or lesson. So one of the things is that one takes into account the basic kharma of the race to which one is coming. One comes to a race whose kharma is suitable for increasing one's opportunities for doing the allotted task. Apart from that race kharma doesn't affect one because it is more to do with the Manu of the race.

Well now, Ester Moray has another question here. She seems to be a nice young lady so let's spare her a few more minutes, shall we? Her third question is, "What can an individual do to reincarnate with the same family they now have, or is this not possible?"

I have just been telling you how things are planned. So if it is necessary for people to come together in another life then they will come together in another life, and arrangements are made for that specific purpose. You might remember the case of the girl in India; she died as a child, and then she came back as a child to a family who lived just a few miles away, and she kept on talking

195

about her other family. Many enquiries were made, and eventually the two families were brought together, and the reincarnated girl was able to give proof that she had reincarnated. That is a case which is authenticated beyond all possible doubt.

Now, here is a question for you; "Mermen and mermaids—were these truly a race of people and if so what intellect did they possess and what happened to them?"

Actually all that the average person knows about mermaids and mermen goes back to the days of Atlantis. Now, Atlantis was a far more technically accomplished place than this present day civilization.

People could be made, lumps of protoplasm could be formed in somewhat human shape and they were used as servants—not as slaves—they were used as servants because they were people of inferior mentality, they were, in fact, "made" for the purpose of serving their masters and mistresses.

Theoretically nowadays it is possible to increase the mentality of a dog or a horse or something like that by being irradiated by special rays and by being fed special chemicals. In that way the brain voltages can be altered and so the intelligence-factor increased. There is no reason, for instance, why monkeys should not be altered by chemicals so that their mentality is greatly increased and thus they could, in effect, be a sort of servant to people. I know quite recently at the Calgary Stampede procession when we had all manner of things going through the city streets there was one monkey riding a horse, and he was wearing clothes. He was doffing his hat to the onlookers and behaving in every way the same as the humans around him. Except for looks one couldn't have told the difference so far as behaviour was concerned. And that

196

old monkey, he certainly got a lot of applause, too. But then the applause upset his self-control because he jumped off the horse and jumped at the spectators and he was horribly affectionate with them, and it was quite a task, I understand, to get him back on his horse again!

"You mention that in the astral world we can have families. Do we leave them for awhile to attend class on Earth and then return to them at the end of our Earth class?"

Yes, that is quite possible. You may say that we spend twenty-four hours a day on Earth. Certainly we do, but they are Earth hours and time in the astral world is utterly different from the time on Earth, in fact in some of the Hindu books there are stories of people going away from the Earth and spending a little time in the astral and then on their return to Earth finding that a thousand years of Earth time has passed. So it is perfectly feasible for a person to come to Earth and do all manner of things by day, but the person has to sleep and during the sleep the astral bodies go back to the astral world NO MATTER WHETHER PEOPLE REMEMBER IT OR NOT, and the time they spend in the astral world with their families may be perhaps twice as long as they stay on Earth by day. It is all a question of the difference in time.

This next question makes me wonder if some poor soul has been brought up the hard way because the question is: "If a child were pushed through college in his life by a hard-hearted parent would it necessarily help the child in his or her successive lives?"

Oh dear, dear, I am so sorry to have to disappoint you, but the answer is "Yes." Everything we learn, everything we experience is worthwhile and it is saved. Now, a better way to explain it would perhaps be to say that when we go over to the Other Side we take all the good that we have learned on Earth, and all the bad (the dross) is left behind. It's like if you are melting a metal, if you are melting gold, for instance, or silver; well, you melt the stuff and then sludge forms on the top (because gold or silver is heavier than sludge), it forms as a dirty mass which is skimmed off and thrown away leaving the gold or the silver to be poured into ingots. Well, we are in much the same state. All that which we have learned which is of use to the Overself and to our development is retained. The bad is discarded like a bad memory.

People are interested in the astral, aren't they? So here is another one about the astral. It is, "If I were able to astral travel consciously and my wife had been trying without success: 1) Could I evaluate from the astral what she was doing wrong and help her to correct the situation? 2) Would it in any way be wrong to help in this manner?"

The answer is that of course you can go into the astral and find out what the problem is, and of course you can come back and tell her what the problem is. But I can tell you what the problem is now; it is just a matter of memory. She does astral travel. Knowing who you are (and not telling!) I know that your wife has been to see me in the astral, and so have you and you made a big splash about it, too! But your wife is trying too hard, or she may have a little fear. But if she would only take things quietly and not make such efforts then she would remember the astral travels that she did.

Now, here is a bit more which really relates to the Hollow Earth. "Since the publication of your books I would imagine that the Chinese have tried to find the passageways in the mountain and the underground river.

How could it remain so well hidden from such an intensive search?"

The answer is, through masterly misdirection. If you see a blank wall ahead of you and all your tests, including the use of special detectors, etc., convince you that the wall is solid, then you turn elsewhere, and the wall is indeed very well protected because if one goes down far enough one gets to an outpost of the Hollow Earth. You further ask about the approximate date of the underground tunnels. Well, I should say about a million years, or so, ago because they were made well before Atlantis, they were made when first people "went underground", and into the inner world. In passing let me say that although a lot of people will screech with laughter at the thought of a Hollow Earth, let me remind them that for centuries and centuries people thought that the Earth was flat, and if any body had dared to say that the Earth was round then they would have been taken as insane people because—they would have said—if the world is round how can we stand on it, what about the people on the other side of the Earth, they would fall off for sure. We know otherwise, don't we? We know the Earth is round and not flat. Some of us know that the world is hollow, too. Think of that, will you?

Respected Sir, you have got your facts mixed up somewhere or dropped a brick or you haven't been reading my books properly. You say, "Why would a race of people from far out in space want to colonize with the people of this world to produce the Race of Tan?

Well, who said there was going to be a colony coming from beyond space? Just think of this; get all the white people, the yellow people, the red people, the black people, and any other colour or shade you can scrape up, get them all to inter-marry, and look at the result. What would the colour be? Tan, of course. And so we can get the Race of Tan when we get all the peoples of the world inter-marrying because in those days colour will not matter. It doesn't matter in Brasil nowadays. It is one place on the face of this Earth where the black man and the white man work side by side with no thought whatever of colour. I have a very soft spot for Brasil because they are doing well, and it is one of the coming countries. They will be the first to produce citizens for the Race of Tan.

"In 'The Hermit' it was stated that the Gardeners would place someone on this Earth for the hermit to tell his story to. How is it meant that you were placed on this Earth?"

Well, somebody had to be picked, and the person who was picked had to have certain qualifications. For instance, he had to be a very hardy individual, he had to be highly telepathic, highly clairvoyant, he had to have a good memory, and he had to have his personal frequency or wavelength of a certain order. In other words, he had to be constantly in touch with one of the Great Masters. So the poor fellow who did fulfill those qualifications was grabbed and placed in such conditions that he naturally became the listener to the story, and I state that that story is true.

Let's have a statement from Paddle Boat Moffet. He says, "Read the book 'The Spaceships of Ezekiel' by Josef F. Blumrich. You suggested I read it and it proved very interesting and well written." So there you see Paddle Boat Moffet—now a member of the Paddle Boat Club—is able to take advice, to act upon advice, and to profit from advice. He's a good fellow, too.

Here is a question from Wilhem Briceno. He is 18 years of age and he lives in Venezuela. His first question is, "Is there any part of the world in which the original religion taught by Christ is now practised?"

No, I am sorry to say that there is not. Christ departed the scene and for many years the Teachings of Christ were let lapse. But after a number of years a gang of people thought they would start something which would give them some power. Really the early founders of the Christian Church, as it was then, were a lot of cultists, they did not teach that which Christ taught, but they taught that which increased their own power. For example, most of the bunch were paralysed with fright at the thought of women. Christ did not teach that women were unclean. Mind you, I'm sure Christ would not have liked that Women's Libber person who writes to me. But Christ taught that women had rights just as men have rights, but the founders of the church in the year 60 did not want women to get any power at all so it was taught that women had no souls, women were unclean (some of them are by the amount of stuff they put on their face!) However, to answer the question, no, on no place at all of this Earth is the original Teaching of Christ followed.

"Is there in existence now the original version of the Bible? If not, what can one do to enable Christianity to be taught as it was originally intended to be taught?"

Well, if we could find the original version of the Bible we could still not return to basic Christianity because the Bible is just a collection of books consisting of "the Gospel According to . . .", and as I have been saying the Bible is not necessarily the Teachings of Christ. Most of the people in Christ's time couldn't write, anyway.

"If animals are all so intelligent why don't they make temples and houses, and why don't they leave any culture in history?"

But are you sure they don't? You see, it doesn't mean

that a person is civilized or intelligent because one builds a temple or church. I've got one in front of me now which is a concrete monstrosity done in the form of an Indian wig-wam, that is, tent shaped with three imitation poles sticking up from the roof. It's a church all right, but in the form of a tepee, which was a tent of the Indians who, anyway, weren't Christians. So how is there any symbolism in that?

To my own definite knowledge animals are intelligent, but their intelligence takes a different form from that of humans. Humans seem to want to build great buildings so that some other humans can come along and drop bombs on it or shell the cities which humans make. I never understand people who think that humans are the Lords of Creation. They are not. On this particular world admittedly they dominate by force, but do you know that only humans and spiders commit rape? No other animals at all do.

You say about building things, but how about the bees, how about the ants? They have very wonderful civilizations. Ants have fortresses, they have a very effective army, they have cleaners—street cleaners—they have nursemaids and all the rest of it, they even have their "milk cows" which are aphids.

Animals are here for their own particular purpose and for their own particular evolution, and I know from my own personal intensive studies that animals can be highly intelligent, some more intelligent than humans. I say that with a full sense of responsibility and unless you are clairvoyant and telepathic, as I am, then you cannot truthfully contradict me because you would be like a person who was born blind and who would say that there were no such colours as red, green, yellow, etc., etc. Unless you have the same abilities as I have, then you cannot dispute what my superior abilities enable me to know.

In the same way, I cannot walk so it's useless for me to argue with you if you say that it's a very pleasant thing walking over such-and-such a surface. I wouldn't know. I know my own subjects.

Rosemary—that is the only name of her's I have here—writes to me and says, "In your next book would it be possible for you to dwell a little on the causes of a dual personality? You see, I have a dual personality. Does that mean I have great difficulty in following the Middle Way? I tend to go to extremes."

No, Rosemary, it doesn't mean that you are any different from anyone else. It means that you came here to overcome certain defects, and so that you could see what it was like you came as a dual personality. I assume that in a previous life, perhaps in your very last life even, you could not get on with people, and somebody said you couldn't get on with yourself. So, in effect, you said, "All right, I'll go back to Earth as a dual personality and you'll see how well I do!"

A dual personality is just one who has an astrological make-up which causes them to see two sides of the coin at once, surely quite a feat, but it doesn't mean you are any better or any worse than anyone else.

It might even mean that it was intended that you should be twins, you know, identical twins where one egg divides, but for some reason the egg did not divide, and in that case you get a form of dual entity inside one body. Never mind, Rosemary, I will tell you here and now that you are doing very well indeed and there is not the slightest reason why you should be worried so—don't be!

We've got time for one more question, I think, and this

is from Mr. Howard G. Marsh. I get quite a lot of people writing to me from Idaho. All right, Mr. Marsh, you say, "You mention in one of your books that a person has to come back to Earth for every sign of the zodiac. This would be twelve times if he learned his lessons well. Am I correct?"

Mr. Marsh, I have to tell you that you are not correct! A person has to come back and live through every sign of the zodiac and through every quadrant (30 degrees) of every sign of the zodiac, and he has to keep coming back until he accomplishes his task SUCCESSFULLY in every sign and quadrant of that zodiac. So if he is a slow learner he might come to Earth a thousand or two thousand times, which makes it all a bit monotonous, doesn't it?

The tape is spinning on, the day is drawing to a close. Twilight will soon be upon us. The pages of this book are mounting up and the words of its total are exceeding that which is considereed necessary for this book. Before me I have questions—questions—questions—piles of questions, questions enough for many more books to come. And— who knows?—I might yet write another book, there's life in the old man yet. I can still twitch a little, I am still able to push a recorder button. So if you do want another book you know how to get it; all you have to do is to write to my publisher and tell him you want another book by Lobsang Rampa.

For the present, then, I will take leave of you and in doing so bring this book, "Twilight", to its end.

THE END

T. LOBSANG RAMPA

is the author of fourteen extraordinary books, each one immensely readable and thought provoking:

THE SAFFRON ROBE: The personal story of Lobsang Rampa's boyhood at the great Lamasery of Potala.   35p

LIVING WITH THE LAMA: More details of Lobsang Rampa's extraordinary existence—this time from a different angle.   35p

THE THIRD EYE: A great bestseller wherever it has been published. This tells how Lobsang Rampa was given the power of the Third Eye.   35p

DOCTOR FROM LHASA: In which Lobsang Rampa proved that mortal man can discipline his mind and body to survive starvation and torture.   40p

THE RAMPA STORY: Revealing other aspects of the author's strange life and the mystic powers with which he is endowed.   40p

WISDOM OF THE ANCIENTS: A book of Knowledge with special sections on breathing exercises and diet.   40p

YOU—FOREVER: A special course of instruction in psychic development and metaphysics.   35p

THE CAVE OF THE ANCIENTS: Lobsang Rampa's story of his experiences at the Lamaseries of Tibet.   50p

CHAPTERS OF LIFE: Predictions and comments on the events taking place in the astral world.   Illustrated 40p

BEYOND THE TENTH: Lobsang Rampa explores the spiritual potential inherent in every human being.   35p

FEEDING THE FLAME: In his first ten books Lobsang Rampa has tried to light a candle, or possible two. In this, the eleventh book, he is trying to feed the flame.   50p

THE HERMIT: A young monk receives the wisdom of the ages from an old, blind hermit.   35p

THE THIRTEENTH CANDLE: Lobsang Rampa answers questions about the world of the astral, healing, life after death and many more.   35p

CANDLELIGHT: More questions answered about aspects of metaphysics—pendulums, dowsing, levitation and teleportation, etc.

ALL AVAILABLE IN CORGI BOOKS

JOURNEYS OUT OF THE BODY
by ROBERT A. MONROE

Every night billions of people undergo an experience which they do not understand but without which they cannot survive—that is the experience of sleep. Nightmares, dreams, the sensation of 'falling'—all are accepted phenomena of sleeping, but what exactly happens to our minds while our bodies are in this peculiar state?

For hundreds of years followers of Eastern religions have accepted sleep as a means of escape from the restrictions of our physical bodies—a time when our spirit, or astral body, is able to travel in a world unbounded by distance or time. It is this world that Robert Monroe explores in *Journeys out of the Body*. In a step by step account he describes his first frightening experience when he realised his abilities, and also gives detailed instructions on how to initiate an 'out-of-body' experience . . .

0 552 09531 1—**40p**   T215

BEYOND EARTH: MAN'S CONTACT WITH UFO's
by RALPH BLUM with JUDY BLUM

Millions of people believe they have seen them . . .
Millions of people claim to have heard them . . .
'They have caused car ignitions to fail and radios to cut out . . .

'They' are the UFO's—unidentified flying objects. And in every country in the world, reliable people are seeing and experiencing a phenomenon for which 20th century science has no explanation. Is mankind being studied by a race of superior intelligence to our own? Is Earth the destination for a reconnaissance expedition from some far off galaxy? And who will be next to witness the strange apparitions in our skies?

0 552 09686 5—**50p**   T216

THE SPEAR OF DESTINY
by TREVOR RAVENSCROFT

What motivated a shabby down-and-out to become the most destructive despot the world has ever known? Until recently little was known of the truth behind Hitler's meteoric rise to power from a Vienna flophouse—and what *was* known was deliberately withheld from the public by the authorities at the end of the war. Now, Trevor Ravenscroft reveals for the first time the secret occult background of the Nazi Party; the Satanic supernatural development and faculties of Hitler and the amazing history of the Spear of Longinus—the Spear which pierced the side of Christ—the extraordinary powers invested in it that Hitler employed in his attempted conquest of the world.

552 09609 1—60p   T175

IN SEARCH OF ANCIENT MYSTERIES
by ALAN AND SALLY LANDSBURG

What exists in the small patch of the Atlantic ocean known as the Bermuda triangle which has devoured more than a hundred ships and aircraft during the past two centuries alone?

Why does virtually every culture on Earth contain a legend of a great flood?

Where did ancient civilisations acquire their vast knowledge of astronomy and mathematics?

Why do men think of their gods as looking down from the sky?

Alan and Sally Landsburg found themselves on the trail of these and other strange phenemena when they went
    IN SEARCH OF ANCIENT MYSTERIES

552 09588 5—50p   T176

A SELECTED LIST OF PSYCHIC, MYSTIC
AND OCCULT BOOKS THAT APPEAR IN CORGI

All these books are available at your bookshop or newsagent: or can be ordered direct from the publisher. Just tick the titles you want and fill in the form below.

CORGI BOOKS, Cash Sales Department, P.O. Box 11, Falmouth, Cornwall.
Please send cheque or postal order. No currency, and allow 10p per book to cover the cost of postage and packing (plus 5p each for additional copies).

NAME ....

ADDRESS ....

(APRIL, 75)

While every effort is made to keep prices low, it is sometimes necessary to increase prices at short notice. Corgi Books reserve the right to show new retail prices on covers which may differ from those previously advertised in the text or elsewhere.

not dispute what my superior abilities enable me to know.

In the same way, I cannot walk so it's useless for me to argue with you if you say that it's a very pleasant thing walking over such-and-such a surface. I wouldn't know. I know my own subjects.

Rosemary—that is the only name of her's I have here—writes to me and says, "In your next book would it be possible for you to dwell a little on the causes of a dual personality? You see, I have a dual personality. Does that mean I have great difficulty in following the Middle Way? I tend to go to extremes."

No, Rosemary, it doesn't mean that you are any different from anyone else. It means that you came here to overcome certain defects, and so that you could see what it was like you came as a dual personality. I assume that in a previous life, perhaps in your very last life even, you could not get on with people, and somebody said you couldn't get on with yourself. So, in effect, you said, "All right, I'll go back to Earth as a dual personality and you'll see how well I do!"

A dual personality is just one who has an astrological make-up which causes them to see two sides of the coin at once, surely quite a feat, but it doesn't mean you are any better or any worse than anyone else.

It might even mean that it was intended that you should be twins, you know, identical twins where one egg divides, but for some reason the egg did not divide, and in that case you get a form of dual entity inside one body. Never mind, Rosemary, I will tell you here and now that you are doing very well indeed and there is not the slightest reason why you should be worried so—don't be!

We've got time for one more question, I think, and this

is from Mr. Howard G. Marsh. I get quite a lot of people writing to me from Idaho. All right, Mr. Marsh, you say, "You mention in one of your books that a person has to come back to Earth for every sign of the zodiac. This would be twelve times if he learned his lessons well. Am I correct?"

Mr. Marsh, I have to tell you that you are not correct! A person has to come back and live through every sign of the zodiac and through every quadrant (30 degrees) of every sign of the zodiac, and he has to keep coming back until he accomplishes his task SUCCESSFULLY in every sign and quadrant of that zodiac. So if he is a slow learner he might come to Earth a thousand or two thousand times, which makes it all a bit monotonous, doesn't it?

The tape is spinning on, the day is drawing to a close. Twilight will soon be upon us. The pages of this book are mounting up and the words of its total are exceeding that which is considereed necessary for this book. Before me I have questions—questions—questions—piles of questions, questions enough for many more books to come. And—who knows?—I might yet write another book, there's life in the old man yet. I can still twitch a little, I am still able to push a recorder button. So if you do want another book you know how to get it; all you have to do is to write to my publisher and tell him you want another book by Lobsang Rampa.

For the present, then, I will take leave of you and in doing so bring this book, "Twilight", to its end.

THE END

T. LOBSANG RAMPA

is the author of fourteen extraordinary books, each one immensely readable and thought provoking:

THE SAFFRON ROBE: The personal story of Lobsang Rampa's boyhood at the great Lamasery of Potala.   35p

LIVING WITH THE LAMA: More details of Lobsang Rampa's extraordinary existence—this time from a different angle.   35p

THE THIRD EYE: A great bestseller wherever it has been published. This tells how Lobsang Rampa was given the power of the Third Eye.   35p

DOCTOR FROM LHASA: In which Lobsang Rampa proved that mortal man can discipline his mind and body to survive starvation and torture.   40p

THE RAMPA STORY: Revealing other aspects of the author's strange life and the mystic powers with which he is endowed.   40p

WISDOM OF THE ANCIENTS: A book of Knowledge with special sections on breathing exercises and diet.   40p

YOU—FOREVER: A special course of instruction in psychic development and metaphysics.   35p

THE CAVE OF THE ANCIENTS: Lobsang Rampa's story of his experiences at the Lamaseries of Tibet.   50p

CHAPTERS OF LIFE: Predictions and comments on the events taking place in the astral world.   Illustrated 40p

BEYOND THE TENTH: Lobsang Rampa explores the spiritual potential inherent in every human being.   35p

FEEDING THE FLAME: In his first ten books Lobsang Rampa has tried to light a candle, or possible two. In this, the eleventh book, he is trying to feed the flame.   50p

THE HERMIT: A young monk receives the wisdom of the ages from an old, blind hermit.   35p

THE THIRTEENTH CANDLE: Lobsang Rampa answers questions about the world of the astral, healing, life after death and many more.   35p

CANDLELIGHT: More questions answered about aspects of metaphysics—pendulums, dowsing, levitation and teleportation, etc.   40p

ALL AVAILABLE IN CORGI BOOKS

JOURNEYS OUT OF THE BODY
by ROBERT A. MONROE

Every night billions of people undergo an experience which they do not understand but without which they cannot survive—that is the experience of sleep. Nightmares, dreams, the sensation of 'falling'—all are accepted phenomena of sleeping, but what exactly happens to our minds while our bodies are in this peculiar state?

For hundreds of years followers of Eastern religions have accepted sleep as a means of escape from the restrictions of our physical bodies—a time when our spirit, or astral body, is able to travel in a world unbounded by distance or time. It is this world that Robert Monroe explores in *Journeys out of the Body*. In a step by step account he describes his first frightening experience when he realised his abilities, and also gives detailed instructions on how to initiate an 'out-of-body' experience . . .

0 552 09531 1—**40p**   T215

BEYOND EARTH: MAN'S CONTACT WITH UFO's
by RALPH BLUM with JUDY BLUM

Millions of people believe they have seen them . . .
Millions of people claim to have heard them . . .
'They have caused car ignitions to fail and radios to cut out . . .

'They' are the UFO's—unidentified flying objects. And in every country in the world, reliable people are seeing and experiencing a phenomenon for which 20th century science has no explanation. Is mankind being studied by a race of superior intelligence to our own? Is Earth the destination for a reconnaissance expedition from some far off galaxy? And who will be next to witness the strange apparitions in our skies?

0 552 09686 5—**50p**   T216

THE SPEAR OF DESTINY
by TREVOR RAVENSCROFT

What motivated a shabby down-and-out to become the most destructive despot the world has ever known? Until recently little was known of the truth behind Hitler's meteoric rise to power from a Vienna flophouse—and what *was* known was deliberately withheld from the public by the authorities at the end of the war. Now, Trevor Ravenscroft reveals for the first time the secret occult background of the Nazi Party; the Satanic supernatural development and faculties of Hitler and the amazing history of the Spear of Longinus—the Spear which pierced the side of Christ—the extraordinary powers invested in it that Hitler employed in his attempted conquest of the world.

552 09609 1—60p   T175

IN SEARCH OF ANCIENT MYSTERIES
by ALAN AND SALLY LANDSBURG

What exists in the small patch of the Atlantic ocean known as the Bermuda triangle which has devoured more than a hundred ships and aircraft during the past two centuries alone?

Why does virtually every culture on Earth contain a legend of a great flood?

Where did ancient civilisations acquire their vast knowledge of astronomy and mathematics?

Why do men think of their gods as looking down from the sky?

Alan and Sally Landsburg found themselves on the trail of these and other strange phenemena when they went
    IN SEARCH OF ANCIENT MYSTERIES

552 09588 5—50p   T176

A SELECTED LIST OF PSYCHIC, MYSTIC AND OCCULT BOOKS THAT APPEAR IN CORGI

☐ 09471 4	**MYSTERIES FROM FORGOTTEN WORLDS** (illus.)		
		Charles Berlitz	40p
☐ 09556 7	**THE SPACESHIPS OF EZEKIEL** (illus.)	*J.F. Blumrich*	50p
☐ 09392 0	**THE MYSTERIOUS UNKNOWN** (illus.)	*Robert Charroux*	50p
☐ 08800 5	**CHARIOTS OF THE GODS?** (illus.)	*Erich von Daniken*	50p
☐ 09083 2	**RETURN TO THE STARS** (illus.)	*Erich von Daniken*	40p
☐ 09411 0	**GOD DRIVES A FLYING SAUCER**	*R.L. Dione*	30p
☐ 09430 7	**THE UFO EXPERIENCE** (illus.)	*J. Allen Hynek*	50p
☐ 09556 7	**IN SEARCH OF ANCIENT MYSTERIES** (illus.)		
		Alan & Sally Lindsburg	50p
☐ 09232 0	**SECRET OF THE ANDES**	*Brother Philip*	30p
☐ 08880 3	**THE THIRTEENTH CANDLE**	*T. Lobsang Rampa*	35p
☐ 08765 3	**THE HERMIT**	*T. Lobsang Rampa*	35p
☐ 08611 8	**FEEDING THE FLAME**	*T. Lobsang Rampa*	35p
☐ 08408 5	**LIVING WITH THE LAMA**	*T. Lobsang Rampa*	35p
☐ 08105 1	**BEYOND THE TENTH**	*T. Lobsang Rampa*	35p
☐ 07652 x	**CHAPTERS OF LIFE** (illus.)	*T. Lobsang Rampa*	35p
☐ 07349 0	**THE SAFFRON ROBE**	*T. Lobsang Rampa*	35p
☐ 09138 3	**YOU-FOREVER**	*T. Lobsang Rampa*	35p
☐ 07249 6	**WISDOM OF THE ANCIENTS**	*T. Lobsang Rampa*	35p
☐ 07146 3	**DOCTOR FROM LHASA**	*T. Lobsang Rampa*	35p
☐ 07249 4	**THE RAMPA STORY**	*T. Lobsang Rampa*	35p
☐ 07145 5	**THE THIRD EYE**	*T. Lobsang Rampa*	35p
☐ 01320 x	**THE CAVE OF THE ANCIENTS**	*T. Lobsang Rampa*	35p
☐ 09390 4	**CANDLELIGHT**	*T. Lobsang Rampa*	40p
☐ 09609 1	**SPEAR OF DESTINY**	*Trevor Ravenscroft*	60p
☐ 68243 8	**LIMBO OF THE LOST** (illus.)	*John Wallace Spencer*	40p
☐ 65820 0	**THE CONFESSIONS OF ALEISTER CROWLEY** (illus.)		
		ed. John Symonds & Kenneth Grant	80p

All these books are available at your bookshop or newsagent: or can be ordered direct from the publisher. Just tick the titles you want and fill in the form below.

CORGI BOOKS, Cash Sales Department, P.O. Box 11, Falmouth, Cornwall.
Please send cheque or postal order. No currency, and allow 10p per book to cover the cost of postage and packing (plus 5p each for additional copies).

NAME ....

ADDRESS ....

(APRIL, 75) ....

While every effort is made to keep prices low, it is sometimes necessary to increase prices at short notice. Corgi Books reserve the right to show new retail prices on covers which may differ from those previously advertised in the text or elsewhere.